# *Italian–American*
# *Holiday Traditions*

# Italian-American Holiday Traditions

## Celebrations and Family Entertainment

Lori Granieri

CITADEL PRESS
Kensington Publishing Corp.
www.kensingtonbooks.com

CITADEL PRESS books are published by

Kensington Publishing Corp.
850 Third Avenue
New York, NY 10022

All Kensington titles, imprints, and distributed lines are available at special quantity
discounts for bulk purchases for sales promotions, premiums, fund-raising, educational,
or institutional use. Special book excerpts or customized printings can also be created
to fit specific needs. For details, write or phone the office of the Kensington special
sales manager: Kensington Publishing Corp., 850 Third Avenue, New York, NY 10022,
attn: Special Sales Department, phone 1-800-221-2647.

Citadel Press logo Reg. U.S. Patent and Trademark Office
Citadel Press is a trademark of Kensington Publishing Corp.

First printing: August 2002

10 9 8 7 6 5 4 3 2 1

Printed in the United States of America

Library of Congress Control Number 2001099197

ISBN 0-8065-2366-2

To my loving dad, George Bennington Mutz.

Your inspiration and belief in me made me who I am today.

I carry you in my heart.

# Contents

# Preface

THE ITALIAN-AMERICAN CULTURE is rich with tradition, from weekly family get-togethers around the dinner table to extravagant holiday celebrations with festive music, colorful decorations, and meals with as many as fourteen courses. *Italian-American Holiday Traditions* explores the different ways Italian-Americans celebrate the holidays as well as some great ideas for decorating, entertaining, preparing and serving meals, and adding special touches to every occasion.

In writing this book, I explored many avenues related to Italian-American holiday traditions, from the practices that take place in Italy to the many and extremely varied ways they are carried out in the United States.

In gathering information, I drew upon my own family traditions and holiday memories, assorted research conducted over time on the Italian culture, and interviews with and stories contributed by several Italian-Americans across the country.

As food is an important part of the Italian-American culture, especially in celebrations, you will find numerous recipes, many from my family, passed on to me by my mother, grandmother, and several aunts and great-aunts, some ingrained in memory by observing and helping my parents cook over the years as well as my own culinary inventions and several shared by various Italian-Americans. A large portion of the recipes in this book were contributed by the owners of Claro's Italian Market, who provide hundreds of original recipes to their customers.

Throughout this book, you will discover various ideas on types of foods to serve during different holidays, for large dinners around the table as well as for cocktail parties. Recipes at the end of several chapters correspond with many of the traditional foods eaten during those holidays.

Of course, many of the recipes can be served at more than one holiday meal—and at nonholidays as well. I have provided a quick and easy reference at the end of the book. In addition to this general index, you will find a recipe index broken down by category—appetizers, vegetables, seafood, and so forth. Feel free to vary these recipes as you see fit, as much of Italian cooking is not a science but an art, re-created and flavored by each individual cook who changes recipes as he or she chooses.

I have a passion for Italian culture, and I feel fortunate to have inherited the wonderful traditions embraced and bestowed by my family. In addition, my love for cooking, decorating, and party planning (having learned from two excellent cooks and entertainers, my own parents) has made this project a lot of fun and close to my heart.

I hope you will find this book interesting (as a source for learning about traditions), nostalgic (bringing back memories of your own holiday festivities), and useful (providing ideas, tips, and suggestions for decorating, party and meal planning, and recipes). May all your holidays be filled with joy as you celebrate Italian style.

# A calendar of Italian and Italian-American holidays and special events

*January*

   1—New Year's Day
   5—Epiphany Eve, the night to leave
      shoes out for La Befana
   6—Epiphany

*February*

   14—Valentine's Day

*February–March*

   Carnival

*March*

   17—St. Patrick's Day
   19—St. Joseph's Day

*March/April*

   Ash Wednesday
   Lent
   Palm Sunday
   Holy Thursday
   Good Friday
   Holy Saturday
   Easter Sunday
   Easter Monday

*April*

   25—Italian Liberation Day

*May*

   1—May Day and Memorial Day
   Mother's Day (second Sunday)

*June*

   Father's Day (second Sunday)
   13—Feast of St. Anthony of Padua
   24—Feast of John the Baptist

*July*

   4—American Independence Day

*August*

   15—Assumption, also known as
      Ferragosto, the official start of
      the Italian holiday season

*September*

   19—Feast of San Gennaro (Naples)

*October*

   Italian Heritage Month
    4—Feast of St. Francis Assisi
   12—Columbus Day
   31—Halloween

*November*

   1—All Saints' Day
   2—All Souls' Day
   Thanksgiving

*December*

   Advent
    6—St. Nicholas Day
    8—Immaculate Conception
   13—St. Lucia Day
   17—Saturnalia
   24—Christmas Eve
   25—Christmas Day
   26—St. Stephen's Day (Santo Stefano)
   31—New Year's Eve/St. Sylvester's
      Night

*Italian-American*
*Holiday Traditions*

# 1

# An Italian-American Holiday Celebration

THE HOUSE IS WARM, cozy, and inviting. Music is playing loudly but is almost drowned out by the laughter and loud conversation coming from every room. You are overcome by the assortment of scents wafting from the kitchen—the simmering sauce, roasting garlic, baking bread, and percolating coffee.

In the living room, you join your loved ones. Everyone is there—parents, siblings, grandparents, godparents, aunts, uncles, cousins, family friends. People are mingling over festive cocktails and red wine, while snacking from antipasto platters—olives, artichoke hearts, peppers, cheeses, calamari—and dipping focaccia and bread sticks in olive oil, balsamic vinegar, and an array of dips and sauces.

As you enter the dining room, your eyes gravitate toward the artistic and mouthwatering display. There are main courses, side dishes, pastas, soups, salads, vegetables, cheeses, fruits, breads, and wines. A separate table is devoted to sweets in all shapes, colors, and sizes.

You take your place at the long table and join in for a prayer of thanks, which is followed by a toast and a simultaneous *"Salude"* as wineglasses are raised. Then, several rounds of serving platters are passed around the table, and as the food is circulating, your culinary adventure begins. Spectacular Italian dishes that have been in the family for generations bring back memories of childhood.

After an hour or two of indulging in these culinary delights, you push yourself away from the table, ignoring that last third of an Italian cookie lying alone on your plate, and vow to fast for at least a couple of days.

The men disappear to the basement for a game of cards. The kids run off to play. The women clear the table, clean the dishes, and prepare bags for guests to take home. Afterward the women sit in the kitchen conversing over coffee. Sometime after midnight, all the guests go home.

You are very pleased to have been part of another holiday celebration. And you're thankful to be Italian-American with your strong family ties and the traditions that have been passed down from generation to generation.

❧

This is an example of a typical Italian-American holiday celebration. It could have been just about any holiday—Thanksgiving, Christmas, or Easter—with many of the features distinctive of Italian-American festivities. Of course, celebrations vary from family to family, household to household, community to community, expressing the wide range of backgrounds, tastes, and preferences of the diverse Italian-American population.

Throughout this book, we will explore the many holiday traditions that take place in the homes of Italian-Americans everywhere. We will look at the customs associated with each holiday, from how they originated and have been celebrated in Italy through the years to the influences of American life and how we celebrate today.

We will examine the lives of many Italian-Americans, from those who were born and raised in Italy and recently became American citizens to those whose great-grandparents migrated here many years ago and are very assimilated into the American way of life.

Included will be examples of how various families celebrate all of the holidays considered important in the Italian-American culture. Of course, these include Christmas and Easter, which are observed worldwide, as well as occasions that aren't necessarily embraced by all cultures, but bear great significance to many Italians, like St. Joseph's Day, Epiphany and many saints' feast days, and American holidays like Thanksgiving, to which Italian-Americans add their own touches. Also included will be Columbus Day, considered an important event in much of the Italian-American culture, as well as several religious days of obligation, including All Saints' Day and Immaculate Conception.

You will hear from several Italian-American men and women as they share their families' holiday celebration stories and memories of traditional Christmases, Easters, and other feast days. Also featured are recipes and suggestions for fabulous feasts to serve on every special occasion, along with decorating tips, special touches, ideas for fun projects, activities, crafts, things to do with kids, and more.

We will go over every aspect needed to plan, prepare, and present fabulous holiday celebrations throughout the entire year—authentic, chic, contemporary, and unique, as well as meaningful, memorable, and full of fun!

## Italian-American Holidays Explored

The Italian-American holiday season really gets under way with the onset of fall. Some Italian-Americans recognize October as Italian Heritage Month, which in many cities is celebrated with parades, festivals, and educational programs. Many also celebrate Columbus Day on October 12 (or the closest Monday), during which more cultural events are planned.

In the beginning of November we celebrate two religious feasts—All Saints' Day, to honor the many saints who might not have specific feast days assigned to them, and All Souls' Day, to honor our loved ones no longer with us. In the Italian tradition, there are special rituals and even recipes associated with these holy days, such as baking small bean-shaped cookies (called *fave dei morti*, "dead man's beans") on All Souls' Day.

Thanksgiving, while not a holiday celebrated in Italy, is embraced wholeheartedly by Italian-Americans. It is another day devoted to being with loved ones and preparing an enormous feast. Some people add Italian touches with such dishes as *ravioli con la zucca* (pumpkin ravioli), along with pasta side dishes and Italian desserts. We will look at ideas for table settings, activities and crafts for kids, and various side dishes and desserts that make great additions to Thanksgiving Day celebrations.

Immediately after Thanksgiving, the Christmas season begins. Christmastime is by far the most festive time of year for Italian-Americans. In addition to Christmas Eve and Christmas Day, which are huge celebrations with many Italian traditions, the season features several other feast days.

Many Italian-Americans observe some of the important pre-Christmas holidays observed in Italy, including the Feast of the Immaculate Conception on December 8 and the Feast of Santa Lucia on December 13 (known in Palermo for serving panelli, deep-fried chickpea pancakes). Some also recognize December 6 as the celebration of the birth of San Nicola, the original St. Nicholas.

Perhaps the biggest Italian-American celebration (as in Italy) is Christmas Eve, which often features a fish dinner—sometimes seven, ten, or twelve courses of fish, plus pastas, breads, and desserts—and usually concludes with Midnight Mass. Some popular Christmas Eve dinners include *baccala*, *capitone* (eel), squid, smelt, octopus, clams, shrimp, lasagna, and spaghetti. (Note: It is said that a seven-fish-course dinner represents the seven sacraments or gifts of the Holy Ghost.)

Other Italian Christmas touches include the burning of the Yule log, listening to music of the *Piferari* (bagpipers), the construction of a *Ceppo* (a pyramid-shaped wooden frame with three tiers showcasing a manger scene, fruits, candy, and presents), elaborate Nativity scenes and villages, and a *presepio* (which is a more elaborate shrine to the Holy Child around which everyone gathers to pray). The house is filled with pine, lights, Christmas tapers, and oranges and tangerines, which provide a wonderful fragrance.

Chestnuts are roasting, Tombola (a card game similar to Bingo) is played, and the story of Christmas is told.

The sweets are a tradition themselves: *struffoli, spumetti, mostaciolli, torrone, pignulata, cassada*, cannoli, fig cookies, and sweet breads like *pandoro, panforte, pandolce*, and panettone. In fact, many Italian-American women will devote an entire day (or more) to getting together and baking up to twenty different types of Italian cookies.

In the Italian tradition, there are twelve days of Christmas—from

Christ's birthday to the feast of the Epiphany on January 6. Saint Stephen's Day is celebrated by some on December 26. For many, the Epiphany (when the three Wise Men arrived in Bethlehem) is a very important holiday filled with special foods, visits to relatives, and a visit from La Befana (a friendly witch who brings gifts to Italian children). Many families eat *pinza* (rustic sweet bread) and drink *vin brulé* (hot mulled wine).

In this book, several chapters are devoted to Christmas and its many components. After an explanation of the many holidays associated with Christmas, both as they take place in Italy and as many of those traditions are celebrated here today by various individuals who share their stories, we will explore ways to get the house ready for the holidays, creating the ambience, ideas for decorating and entertaining, spreading holiday cheer, unique gift and gift-wrapping ideas, and fun activities to plan with family and friends from great holiday parties to exciting outings. Lots of how-tos will be provided for Christmas crafts and decorations. Christmas food will be discussed in detail, and there are various menus to serve on Christmas Eve and Christmas Day, along with recipes and suggestions.

New Year's Eve is a festive time as well, with traditional foods and practices. New Year's Eve and New Year's Day ideas will be shared, with recipes and party ideas. We will explore New Year's traditions as they are carried out in Italy. New Year's Eve is also the Feast of St. Sylvester, who was pope when Constantine declared Christianity the official state religion of Italy. It is believed that St. Sylvester closes the door on one year and its pagan ceremonies and opens it on a new one in a Christian era.

Springtime brings with it a whole new season of celebrations. St. Joseph's Day, on March 19, is a major holiday for many Italian-Americans, who will prepare an abundance of meatless foods (because it falls in Lent) including the popular *zeppole* pastry, *sfinge* (or *sfinci*), and breads made in dozens of different shapes. Many also construct an altar of three levels draped in linens and adorned with flowers and decorative breads.

The Easter season features a month of feast days and holy days, many of which are observed in church. We will explore Ash Wednesday, Palm Sunday, Holy Thursday, Good Friday, Holy Saturday, and of course, Easter Sunday. In addition, we will examine the season of Lent and the Catholic beliefs and practices associated with it. (Some Italian-Americans celebrate the beginning of Lent on Shrove Tuesday, which in Venice kicks off Carnival, with Mardi Gras parties and *sfinge* pastries.)

Easter is celebrated with many traditional foods, including lamb, hard-boiled eggs, Easter breads, *pandolce*, and ricotta pie. Easter Monday *(Pasquetta)* is celebrated with picnics and, again, lots of food. Included in this chapter will be stories, recipes, and ideas for decorations and activities.

Several saints' and other feast days are observed throughout the year by Italians throughout the world, including Assumption and St. John's, San Gennaro's, St. Anthony's, and St. Francis's feast days. Included will be backgrounds on the saints, why they are celebrated and by whom (the city or part of Italy of which they are patron saints), along with special recipes associated with them. For example, St. John's Day, June 24, is celebrated with Nocino (a walnut-flavored liqueur), *bruschetta*, pasta, sausage, pork ribs, and snails. St. Anthony (of Padua) is honored on June 13 with songs written for the saint and with St. Anthony bread.

Most Italian-American families set aside one day of the week for a big family get-together. At these dinners, usually held on Sunday, a large meal featuring some sort of pasta is served. We will hear from various individuals about this family tradition and explore different meal ideas.

We will look at Mother's and Father's Days as they are celebrated by Italian-Americans. Included will be the importance of parents and family in Italian culture and how parents are honored on their special days as well as throughout the year. We will explore ideas for meals, parties, and gifts for moms and dads.

Finally, we will explore many ways to add Italian touches to other celebrations, such as birthdays, dinner parties, Valentine's Day, and anniversaries.

The way each of these holidays is celebrated varies from family to family, although you will see lots of similarities when it comes to some.

## Who Are Italian-Americans?

Anyone who identifies with the Italian culture and makes it a part of his or her life is Italian-American. You might be a hundred percent Italian by way of both parents. Perhaps you were even born in Italy. Or you might be half, a fourth, even a tenth Italian. What matters most is your desire to hold on to, learn about, and celebrate your heritage.

Growing up in a family that fully embraced its Italian roots, I learned a lot about the meaning of family and the importance of carrying on tradition. Although my roots do not extend exclusively from Italy—some stem from England, France, and Germany—the cultural heritage I most identify with is Italian.

My maternal grandfather's parents and siblings were born in Naples, Italy, and moved to America, where he, Tony Marino, was born shortly thereafter. Settling in Akron, Ohio, my grandpa and his siblings grew up and started families of their own. In the early 1960s, my grandpa moved his family to California, and soon many of his relatives followed.

They settled in the San Gabriel Valley in southern California. Even though their neighborhood wasn't quite as "Italian" as the ones back east, Grandpa was determined to keep the Italian traditions very much alive. And that he did.

My dad grew up in East Los Angeles and had a very mixed cultural background, none of which he identified with completely. His last name was of German origin—although he did have some Italian blood from his father's mother's side. It didn't take him long to adopt my mom's family's Italian culture, however. He became the most Italian American I ever knew—traveling to Italy, listening to Italian music, cooking exquisitely, and celebrating the holidays with passion. He even made sure to greet and say good-bye to loved ones with three kisses—one cheek, the other cheek, and back to the first cheek.

When my younger brother and I were young children we didn't know what it meant to be Italian. We probably just assumed that all families lived the way we did—with lots of relatives and family friends over at the house all the time, always going to dinner at other relatives' homes, parents who entertained large groups of people every weekend, and celebrating every holiday with lots of food, noise, and activity.

We would later find out that what we had was pretty extraordinary and a part of our cultural heritage.

In my family, celebrations took place throughout the entire year, with get-togethers for just about everything. There were birthday dinners for every relative, Sunday family feasts, and, of course, the holidays! There were many holidays!

There were also barbecues, picnics, and dinner and cocktail parties that took place seemingly for no reason at all. There were always reasons to get together.

My parents loved to entertain, and they did it well. Their house eventually became the "regular meeting place" where most celebrations took place. Both of my parents loved to cook and were great at it. My mom specialized in authentic Italian cuisine—her manicotti, stuffed shells, meatballs, and Crock-Pot chicken cacciatore are the best! My dad was a master griller (he loved his barbecue) and could whip up great dishes in a skillet with whatever ingredients he happened to find. Their kitchen was always fully stocked.

My mom has always loved the holidays and found creative ways to entertain. Dad was her right-hand man, pulling off the materialization of her ideas. Together they were the perfect party-planning team—shopping, planning, cooking, and carrying out memorable get-togethers.

I saw how much fun my parents had entertaining. I watched them planning the menu, getting the house ready for company, and preparing various recipes. I was often elected to go with one of them to the market and to help make the house neat.

Our grandparents never came over empty-handed. Mimi would arrive carrying a side dish, dessert, and one of her little dogs. Grandpa had a bottle of wine in one hand, and the other hand was reaching into his pocket to toss us kids candy and money. When we were little, we called him "the Candy Man."

Once the guests were there, everyone would convene in my parents' kitchen/den area at the kitchen counter. There, they would drink wine and nibble on an assortment of appetizers. Some would gather outside on the patio and others on the sofas in the family room. Dinner was usually served in the dining room or on the patio.

Even on off nights, when there was no dinner party planned, it could almost be guaranteed that someone would drop in and be convinced to stay for dinner.

As I interviewed and gathered stories from a wide variety of Italian-Americans about their own families' traditions, I learned that many celebrated much like my own family. I talked to a wide range of people, varied in age, occupation, and lifestyle, who lived all over the United States. Their ancestors came from all over Italy—every city and region. Some are fully connected with their Italian roots and make sure to carry out every tradition; others are more removed but have very specific childhood memories of certain traditional holidays and still hold on to one or two customs.

What they all have in common are great memories of Italian holiday celebrations. They all take pride in their cultural heritage and love the holidays and the festivities they bring—the huge joyful get-togethers with family and the delicious feasts.

## Where Italian-American Holiday Traditions Come From

Many of our Italian-American holiday traditions stem directly from the various Italian regions and cities from which our ancestors came. In Italy, holidays are celebrated with fervor and often involve the whole town. Parades, street fairs, and public celebrations are held throughout Italy all year long in honor of religious holidays and patron saints and as tributes to national sporting and culinary events. Region to region, city to city, there is a festival of some sort going on almost every day.

While many holiday traditions are practiced all over Italy, some are specific to different regions, especially when it comes to the types of foods served. These variations are reflected in the ways Italian-Americans celebrate. For example, the more southern the region from which your family comes, the more likely it is for fish to be on the menu. However, a lot of these regional distinctions have melded together because of the impact of American life.

Italians who relocated to America brought many of their celebrations with them, coloring their new homes with touches of Italy. Descendents have since taken over in keeping these traditions alive and preserving them for future generations. This is especially apparent in communities heavily populated by Italian-Americans, such as New York's Little Italy; Hoboken, New Jersey; Chicago; and San Francisco. Italian-American clubs and organizations across the country host several holiday events throughout the year as well.

## Where the Holidays Are Celebrated

In many Italian-American families there is one home in which most (or all) of the holiday celebrations are held. This is often the home of the matriarch and patriarch—the ones who are in charge of keeping the traditions alive. They often inherit this role from the former central family, usually their parents, and take on the responsibility with pride. They are also often the ones who have the biggest home, are centrally located, and enjoy cooking and entertaining the most.

Where the holidays are going to be held is typically known way in advance, and it's usually a place that's very comfortable, where everyone feels at home. It is the place that becomes engraved in our memories of family holiday celebrations.

## Why the Holiday Traditions Are Important

In keeping the traditions of our ancestors we are celebrating our culture and connecting with who we are and where we are from. It's a great way to add more meaning to the special moments in our lives and to revel in the happy times. As long as we continue to practice the customs of our heritage, we ensure their survival and a chance for our children and grandchildren to experience a rich part of life. Therefore, we must hold on to our Italian roots through the Italian-American holiday traditions we carry out throughout the year.

# 2

# *Autumn and the Italian-American Holidays*

THE ONSET OF FALL brings a change in the weather that can be dramatic or subtle, depending on where you live. In southern California, the change is on the subtle side, but it's noticeable nonetheless. The intense heat of the late summer brings a longing for cool and breezy. And as far as I'm concerned, that means mid-October through late November. Along with cool and breezy come warm and snuggly—fireplaces, candles, hot chocolate, cappuccino, espresso, stews, rich sauces, slow-cooked roasts, fluffy blankets, staying inside, and curling up with loved ones.

In my family, fall always signified the beginning—of the holiday cycle and the fun! And this is the beginning of the holiday season for many Italian-Americans. For us, a big reason was that most of our birthdays take place in October and November, so these months were filled with extra celebratory events. Right after the last birthday in November, which was my dad's, came Thanksgiving. And as soon as it was done, Christmas season was here.

All Saints' Day and All Souls' Day, which are observed by many Italians around the world, take place in the fall. As a child in Catholic elementary school, I became familiar with both. But at home, Halloween was much more exciting. And while Halloween is not an Italian holiday,

many Italian-Americans participate in its revelry. In fact, many of the customs associated with Halloween are rooted in All Souls' Day.

For many Italian-Americans, October is a time to celebrate Columbus Day with all sorts of festivities. October is also a time to commemorate our heritage.

# Italian Heritage Month

Fittingly, as we get ready to kick off the Italian-American holiday season, October just so happens to be Italian Heritage Month. In various cities throughout the U.S., special events take place during the month to celebrate the contributions and culture of Italians in the United States. At first, Italian heritage was celebrated for a week in May. It was later extended to a month to accommodate the many events that take place, and was then moved to October to coincide with Columbus Day celebrations.

When it comes to Italian Heritage Month celebrations, the whole community gets involved, with programs and activities taking place at libraries, public schools, concert and banquet halls, colleges, restaurants, and on the streets. Activities include book and visual displays, exhibits, performances, concerts, Italian music and radio programs, Italian language classes, lectures on various Italian topics, parades, and festivals.

New York has been honoring Italian Heritage Month since 1976 and has featured month-long celebrations ever since. With themes like "The Legacy of Italy's Artistic and Cultural Contributions to the World," "Italy and Its Regions (*L'Italia delle Regioni*)," and "Italians Reaching Out: Antonio Meucci, Inventor of the Telephone, and Mother Cabrini, Missionary of the Immigrants," Italian New Yorkers honor the accomplishments and positive influences of their ancestors. Activities include lectures, exhibits, concerts, and proclamations.

According to the Italian-American Heritage Month Committee, a collaboration of Italian-American organizations in Massachusetts, the purposes of Italian-American Heritage Month are education and celebration. Their goal is to inform the public about the contributions Italians and

Italian-Americans have made to civilization, specifically in the arts, the humanities, and the sciences. The aim is to "celebrate the impact that Italian culture and language have had and continue to have on our lives as Italian-Americans."

According to their proclamation:

These purposes are realized by encouraging and supporting events and activities throughout the year, but principally during the month of October, that bring people of goodwill together to gain a greater appreciation for the roles played by Italians and Italian-Americans in shaping our civilization.

We view culture in its broadest sense to include an appreciation of the significance and value of the Italian and Latin languages, Italian and Italian-American history, art, architecture, agriculture, cuisine, fashion, film, government, industry, literature, music, religion, science, sport, and all those other aspects of life we view as part of culture. We also will endeavor to bring new perspectives to the lives and times of notable persons of Italian ancestry throughout the ages.

We are committed to be fair and accurate in our portrayals of peoples and events. We appreciate that in many cases persons of Italian or Italian-American ancestry who acquired great power, influence, or wealth caused harm and anguish to others. We also take great pride in the knowledge that without the contributions of Italians and Italian-Americans the world as we know it might not exist, and our cultural life would be immeasurably poorer. And, we recognize that in many cases, especially with respect to certain historical figures, uncertainty exists about what judgment should be made about their conduct or the ideas they espoused. We believe that in all cases freedom of thought and expression must be respected, and we encourage vigorous debate about such matters.

In view of our purposes, we have a special obligation to encourage young people to participate in these events and activities because an awareness of cultural differences is an integral part

## Ideas for Celebrating Italian Heritage Month

- Sample an assortment of Italian music from such musicians as Giuseppe Verdi, Pavarotti, and Frank Sinatra.
- Take an Italian cooking or language class.
- Plan a trip to Italy.
- Make a huge Italian dinner and invite all your friends and relatives.
- Learn more about Italian contributors and discuss their accomplishments with your kids.
- Research your Italian genealogy.
- Join an Italian-American association.
- Find out if any events connected with Italian Heritage Month are happening in your community and attend.

of the educational process, and vital to an understanding that respect for the differences between individuals and groups is the bond that holds our society together. Thus, we believe that the observance of Italian-American Heritage Month must be inclusive of all members of the community, and that the celebration of our cultural identity will serve to reaffirm the importance of celebrating the cultural identities of all other people.*

The best way to celebrate Italian Heritage Month is by learning more about the Italian culture. There are several books available for adults and children on every aspect of Italy, Italians, and Italian-Americans from history to music to famous explorers to literature to language and art.

Visit museums and art galleries that contain works by Italian and

------

*Reprinted with permission from the Committee to Observe October as Italian-American Heritage Month.

Italian-American artists, or areas such as Little Italy in New York and Chicago, or San Francisco's North Beach (formerly Little Italy). Go to the Culinary Institute of America's Colavita Center for Italian Food and Wine in Hyde Park, New York. You will find a Tuscan market display, antipasto bar, wood-fired oven, exhibition kitchen, and a glass wall containing thousands of bottles of Italian wines. Try new Italian restaurants and shop at Italian markets. Buy an Italian cookbook and try a new recipe.

To teach children about the Italian culture, create a huge jigsaw puzzle map of Italy, and let them place the cities in their appropriate places on the map. In addition, do a little research and include some interesting facts about each city on the back of the puzzle piece.

# Columbus Day

Columbus Day is not celebrated by most Italians in Italy or Italian-Americans who have only recently come to the United States, but it is embraced by many Italian-Americans who have lived in the States for many years. Originally celebrated on October 12, the anniversary of Christopher Columbus's arrival in the New World, Columbus Day is now honored on the second Monday in October.

## A Brief History of Columbus Day

Christopher Columbus was born in Genoa, Italy, in 1451. He was convinced that the world was round, not flat as common wisdom held, but was unable to convince his own country to let him prove it. However, Queen Isabella of Spain gave him a chance to find out, and to see if he might discover a new route to China or the East Indies. On August 3, 1492, Columbus and ninety men sailed west on the flagship *Santa Maria*, along with two other ships, the *Niña* and the *Pinta*. Columbus first landed in the New World at San Salvador Island in the Bahamas on October 12, 1492.

Several celebrations took place in honor of Columbus in the late

*Columbus discovered the Caribbean island of St. Lucia on St. Lucy's Day (Santa Lucia), December 13, which is a popular feast day in Italy.*

1700s, the 1800s, and the early 1900s in New York, San Francisco, and Colorado. In 1937, President Franklin D. Roosevelt proclaimed October 12 Columbus Day. In 1971, President Richard Nixon declared Columbus Day a national holiday to be observed on the second Monday of each October.

Columbus Day celebrations feature Italian pasta dinners, a tribute of some sort to Columbus, and a reminder of who he was and what he accomplished. In different parts of the country, there will be Columbus Day parades, festivals, and educational programs. Several are tied in with Italian Heritage Month celebrations, while others are separate.

## Ideas for Columbus Day Celebrations

How can you go about celebrating Columbus Day? Hold a Columbus Day party with an "explorer" theme. Decorate with maps, ships, hidden treasures, and globes. Include an activity that involves a hunt of some sort. (Maybe a big group of friends could discover a new Italian restaurant together.) For a children's party, include hide-and-seek, a scavenger hunt, and crafts, such as making ships. Encourage children to learn more about Columbus and the history of the New World with a trip to the library followed by a discussion. For a fun song related to the theme, tune into Lou Monte's "Please Mr. Columbus (Turn This Ship Around)," found on *The Very Best of Lou Monte*.

Or, throw a party with a traveler theme. Have guests come dressed as tourists or in the style of their favorite travel location. Feature props of suitcases, planes, boats, trains, and motor homes. Have guests bring photos and souvenirs from some of their journeys, or tell stories of travels or great discoveries. Give your traveler party an Italian theme, with costumes, props (miniature gondolas, trains, and scooters for transportation), and food from different Italian destinations.

Maybe you'll have a tailgate party, or go on a hike or walk through town to discover new things. Introduce kids to other concepts of discoveries and being the first to try, make, or find something new. Teach them about such occupations as scientists, paleontologists, detectives, inventors, and artists, as well as about trailblazing Italians and Italian-Americans other than Columbus.

# Religious Italian Holidays in Fall

There are some holy days in the fall that have been an important part of Italian life—in Italy and the United States. All Saints' Day and All Souls' Day, separate yet connected events, are days of obligation in the Catholic Church. And as 90 percent of the Italian population are Roman Catholics, these church feasts are also culturally important.

## All Saints' Day

All Saints' Day is a universal Christian holy day to honor all saints—known and unknown—on November 1. While many saints have individual feast days throughout the year (which we will discuss further in chapter 13), All Saints' Day is an opportunity to celebrate those who do not have a specific feast day. (With so many saints, the Church was unable to give each saint his or her own day, so it designated a common day for all.)

Roman Catholics celebrate All Saints' Day by attending mass and reflecting on the many holy people who once lived. It's a day to remember, thank God, and pray to the saints in heaven that they will help us when we are in need.

When I was a pupil at Sacred Heart Catholic School, All Saints' Day was a major production. All first-through-fourth graders were required to get acquainted with our namesake saint or our favorite saint, go to the school library, check out a book on the saint, and then write a report. Then we had to come up with a costume best portraying that saint and wear it to school on All Saints' Day (or whatever weekday was closest).

Since I didn't have a namesake saint, I always went as Mary, in a long white cotton gown and light blue veil, and carried a rosary. My brother, Daniel, was St. Daniel and carried a stuffed lion. After attending mass, the whole school would meet in the courtyard for a prayer ceremony, followed by an All Saints' Day parade. The older students didn't dress up, but helped facilitate the event.

That was also the day our classrooms had a party—instead of a Halloween party like the public schools had. This was how I became familiar

*Michelangelo's frescoes in the Sistine Chapel were unveiled on All Saints' Day in 1541.*

with the saints and the importance of honoring them. I had no idea at the time that in Italy they had similar celebrations.

I like to think we can extend All Saints' Day as a time to honor all the good, most giving, caring, and "saintly" people in our lives and do something nice for them. Another way to celebrate is to strive to become more like the saints during that day, and do good things to others.

## All Souls' Day

All Souls' Day is said to have its origins in an ancient festival of the dead, and was spread through Europe by St. Odilo of France in the late thirteenth century. It is celebrated on November 2 with masses and celebrations in honor of the dead. It is a time when families fondly remember their deceased members and pray for their souls. Many people also visit their loved ones' graves bearing flowers.

According to the Catholic Church, All Souls' Day is dedicated to praying for those souls in purgatory (where souls go for atonement when they are not quite ready for heaven). The Catholic belief is that there are three levels of being: living here on earth; waiting in purgatory (where the faithful are purified for entry into heaven); and life ever after in either heaven—sainthood—or hell. On All Souls' Day, we pray for those on earth and in purgatory so that they may go to heaven. It is customary to pray six Our Fathers, six Hail Marys, and six Glory Bes to release a soul in purgatory into heaven. To release another soul, one leaves the church building and re-enters to repeat the prayers.

In Italy, November 1 is called *Ognisanti*, and November 2 is *I Morti*. On both days, people visit the graves of their loved ones with flowers (especially chrysanthemums). They will often bring along stools and sit for hours with their dearly departed. Many people will go to a gravesite several days ahead to prepare the area, cleaning the headstone and pruning the weeds around it.

Italians also spend the two holy days attending church services, visiting friends and relatives, and baking traditional foods. Many make small bean-shaped cookies called *fave dei morti* ("dead man's beans"), which at one time were placed on loved ones' graves to ward off evil spirits. They also bake *pane dei morti* ("bread of the dead") and soul cakes, which they sometimes leave out on the night of November 1, lit by candlelight in the belief that their deceased loved ones will eat while they visit that night. Some families prepare a big feast on All Souls' Day and set a place at the table for their dead family members. After dinner, they deliver food to the poor.

Some great ways to honor All Saints' and All Souls' Days are to remember, reflect, honor, and pray. Attending mass, meditating, visiting and bringing flowers to loved ones' gravesites, and visiting living friends and relatives are a few ways to commemorate these days. Write a letter to your departed loved ones or buy or make something memorable in their honor. If you want to add an Italian touch, light some candles in their memory, arrange some chrysanthemums, or bake some *fave dei morti*, *pane dei morti*, or soul cakes.

## Halloween

Though not an Italian holiday, Halloween is celebrated by many Italian-Americans. In my family, we always had a special Halloween dinner that usually consisted of slow-cooked chili, corn bread, and salad. Because we were Italian-Americans, it was another reason to get together as a family for a big meal. When we were kids, we couldn't go trick-or-treating until after dinner.

To add an Italian touch to Halloween, prepare a feast of fall harvest foods and pasta. Mix penne pasta with an assortment of vegetables—zucchini, eggplant, and yellow squash. Serve it with bread in the shapes of pumpkins and other Halloween symbols. For dessert, serve pumpkin tiramisu. You might also prepare a Halloween or fall harvest pizza.

## Recipes for Fall

Perhaps the most important aspect of fall for many Italian-American families is that it signifies the beginning of the magical season just ahead. As autumn approaches, we begin to prepare for the many festivities to come during the next several months. The recipes this time of year start to become more rich and filling, with stews and lots of pasta dishes, breads, and pizzas. Many dishes include fresh fall harvest vegetables, including zucchini, eggplant, and asparagus.

## Pasta With Roasted Vegetables

2 zucchinis, chopped
2 small eggplants, chopped
2 medium onions, quartered and halved again
1 bell pepper, cleaned, seeded, and sliced
1 pound asparagus, chopped

3 tablespoons olive oil
2 tablespoons red wine
1 tablespoon brown sugar
1 package fettuccini, prepared according to directions on package
1 tablespoon Parmesan

Preheat oven to 450 degrees. Toss vegetables with 2 tablespoons olive oil and put in roasting pan. Cook 30 to 45 minutes (or until soft). In a separate bowl, mix 1 tablespoon olive oil, wine, and sugar. Toss vegetables with pasta. Drizzle with sugar mixture. Sprinkle with Parmesan.

## Aunt Leona's Homemade Pizza the Easy Way

*(as told by cousin Lucinda)*

Olive oil
2 loaves frozen bread
2 cups onion, chopped
2 large (24-ounce) cans Italian tomatoes
2 large (24-ounce) cans tomato sauce

Salt, pepper, garlic salt, oregano
1 large ball of mozzarella cheese, grated
1 cup Parmesan cheese, grated
Optional: pepperoni, mushrooms, olives

Oil 2 cookie sheets and spread oil on frozen loaves of bread. Place each loaf on a cookie sheet. Let rise until about 3 times original size (approximately 3 hours). Can be left overnight to thaw and rise. Turn dough over and stretch to size of cookie sheet.

To make the sauce, sauté onions in oil in pot until soft. Crush and add canned tomatoes and tomato sauce. Add salt, pepper, garlic salt, and oregano, to taste. Cook until thick (about 2 to 3 hours). Cool sauce and spread on bread just before baking.

Sprinkle grated mozzarella cheese, Parmesan cheese, and any optional toppings. (Add pepperoni last 5 to 10 minutes.) Bake at 350 to 400 degrees for 20 minutes, or until lightly browned on bottom.

## Neapolitan "Margherita" Pizza

Olive oil  
Pizza dough (make, or buy ready-made)  
3 cups canned tomatoes  
2 cups grated mozzarella cheese  

Salt and pepper, to taste  
1 cup grated Parmesan cheese  
2 tablespoons basil  
1 tablespoon oregano  

Roll dough and place on oiled pan; chop tomatoes and spread on dough; mix mozzarella with olive oil and salt and pepper; sprinkle on pizza; sprinkle Parmesan cheese, basil, and oregano on top and drizzle with olive oil. Bake at 450 degrees for about 15 minutes or until cheese is melted.

## Basic Garlic Bread

2–3 cloves of garlic, chopped  
½ cup butter, softened  

12 dinner rolls, cut in half (or a loaf of French bread cut into thin slices)  

Mix butter and garlic and spread on bread. Wrap in foil and bake at 400 degrees for about 20 minutes, or until hot. For crispier bread, heat in broiler an additional few minutes (not in foil).

## Dad's Garlic Bread

Same as above, but mix butter with ½ cup sour cream, garlic salt, and parsley.

# Fave dei Morti or "Dead Man's Beans"
## (small, bean-shaped cookies)

1 cup flour
1 cup chopped almonds
½ cup sugar
¼ cup pine nuts
1 tablespoon butter
⅓ cup sweet liqueur (amaretto, grappa, brandy)

½ lemon peel, grated
½ orange peel, grated
1 teaspoon cinnamon
2 eggs, beaten
¼ cup powdered sugar
½ teaspoon vanilla

Preheat oven to 350 degrees. In bowl, mix flour, almonds, sugar, vanilla, pine nuts, butter, liqueur, lemon and orange peels, and cinnamon. Roll dough into long strands (about ½ inch thick), break off pieces, and mold them into fava bean shapes. Place them on greased cookie sheet. Brush with beaten eggs. Bake about 20 minutes, or until golden brown. Sprinkle with powdered sugar when still warm.

# Claro's Pumpkin Dump Cake

This recipe can be prepared the night before baking.

2½ cups canned pumpkin
½ teaspoon cloves
1 teaspoon ginger
1 teaspoon salt
2 teaspoons cinnamon
6 eggs

1½ cups sugar
2 cups milk
1 box yellow cake mix
½ cup (1 stick) butter, softened
1 cup chopped walnuts or pecans
Whipped cream or Cool Whip

Mix together the first eight ingredients and pour into a 9-by-13-inch cake pan. In a separate bowl, "crumble" yellow cake mix (dry) with 1 cube softened butter. Sprinkle over the pumpkin mixture. Sprinkle chopped walnuts or pecans on the top. Bake at 350 degrees for 1 hour, or until inserted knife comes out clean. Serve with whipped cream or Cool Whip on top.

# 3

# *Italian-American Thanksgiving*

For most Italian-Americans, Thanksgiving is a time to share a feast with loved ones, which is really the core of any celebration. Many also add Italian touches to the Thanksgiving meal, such as lasagna or other pasta dishes. Others incorporate specialty foods that combine the American Thanksgiving theme with the Italian influence, coming up with such creations as pumpkin ravioli (*ravioli con la zucca*) and a variety of stuffings made with ingredients such as mozzarella, Italian sausage, tomatoes, basil, garlic, and Italian bread.

In my family, Thanksgiving was the first huge feast of the season, one of the "you be there or else" days. It used to take place at my aunt's house, but later became one of the many holidays that took place at my parents'. Everyone had an assigned task—a dish or supplies to bring, a cooking or clean-up duty to do.

We always had the traditional turkey feast, accompanied by Mimi's famous stuffing, mashed potatoes, two gravies (one with giblets and one without), yams, cranberries, green bean casserole, antipasto plate, salad, bread, and wine. For dessert we had pumpkin pie, apple pie, pineapple torte, and Italian cookies with coffee and anisette.

The dining room table would be set (usually by me) with the Christmas tablecloth, napkins, and china, and feature some sort of seasonal centerpiece. In the adjoining living room, the "kids' table" would be set in a similar manner.

Everyone would arrive around noon, sit around the kitchen counter (where everyone always convened) talking and drinking wine and eating appetizers—which could have been chips and veggies and dips, focaccia or pizza, cheeses, and crackers. My mom and dad would always be bustling around the kitchen.

Just before it was time to eat, we all took dishes out to the tables, and one of the men would cut the turkey. Then we all joined at the big table for a prayer of thanks. It was always "Bless Us, Oh Lord," and sometimes everyone at the table would then take turns to say what they were thankful for. Then we passed the food and ate and ate.

Next, some of us headed to the kitchen to do dishes for what seemed like hours. We gathered again at the table for dessert and coffee, during which we also had to write out a Christmas list so everyone would have an idea of what to get people. My mom gathered the lists and subsequently gave copies to everyone else.

The best part of Thanksgiving for us kids was knowing that now we were in the countdown to Christmas. Sometimes there would even be Christmas specials on TV we would watch and get into the spirit. As we got older, it became more about being with family.

## Italian Thanksgiving Remembrances

### Professor Philip J. DiNovo

The most memorable Thanksgiving celebrations of my life were at my paternal grandparents'. It was an Italian Thanksgiving, and in many ways paralleled the Pilgrim celebration: food, family, being together, and lots of communication. What made those Thanksgiving celebrations Italian were the pasta, Italian vegetables, stuffing, and the desserts. As I reflect about it, the tables extending from the kitchen into several rooms, the whole family, and the continuous noise were additional Italian touches. Of course we had the turkey with many of the traditional American-type foods. My grandmother would bow to tradition and prepare the corn, sweet potatoes, and so on. My aunt Mary made delicious pumpkin and apple pies, so we had them too.

My paternal grandfather was a truck farmer, and we had those memorable Italian Thanksgivings on the farm. My grandfather raised turkeys, and a few weeks before Thanksgiving it became very exciting on the farm. Many people came to purchase a turkey. The farm, the turkeys, and the house added up to a setting the Pilgrims would feel at home with. Inside that house it was something else, however. Our Thanksgiving dinner was not sparse, as was the first Thanksgiving; ours was a lavish repast. In the middle of the afternoon, after dinner, we'd walk down the old farm road and enjoy the beauty around us. That was my grandparents' place.

I am sure the Pilgrims would not approve our noisy, big, splashy extravaganza. They would have thought our dinner sinful. They would, however, have approved of our gratitude to God for our many blessings, which was an important part of our celebration. Our dinner would end with Italian coffee and liqueur. It enhanced digestion besides being a staple, our way of saying "It's done; the feast is finished." What a celebration! Being together was important to my grandparents and their nine children. Thanksgiving gave us another reason to be together, and we made the most of it.

My grandparents and parents have gone to their eternal reward. My immediate family celebrates Thanksgiving together. We don't have an Italian Thanksgiving anymore; we have the typical Norman Rockwell Thanksgiving. Since I am the oldest member of my immediate family, I seem to be the only one who can recall Italian-style Thanksgivings. It's a shame, but thank God we do celebrate Christmas with Italian traditions. If I had my way, we would have an Italian Thanksgiving this year. *La festa di tacchino*, the feast of the turkey, isn't the memorable celebration it once was for me. Each Thanksgiving I thank God for all the memories of past Thanksgivings and the fact that all my brothers, sisters, and their families are together to celebrate this beautiful and meaningful holiday. My parents and grandparents, I am sure, are very happy to see us together, as *famiglia*.

### Joyce Spataro

Thanksgiving was the same as everyone else's except we would have some kind of macaroni with the meal. When the family would gather together for a dinner either on a holiday or just to get together before we ate, we would have a toast: for God's blessing, good health, and happiness for all.

### Ginny (Granieri) Craven

Thanksgiving was always consistently the same as far as the amount of food. It was a joke that when our family gathered for any holiday, we always had enough food to feed several armies! And it was very true. Everyone always left with a doggie bag. The turkey was always stuffed with an incredible stuffing (my mom made the best), and we also had mashed potatoes, sweet potatoes, Nanny's or my aunt Patsy's gravy, homemade cranberry sauce, Nanny's homemade bread and rolls, Aunt Gerry's Jell-O mold, a green salad, a fresh vegetable, a relish tray that consisted of Italian olives and pickles, my mom's creamed onions (which were to die for), and of course plenty of desserts, like Nanny's homemade Italian cookies, my aunt Patsy's incredible pecan pie, wonderful pumpkin pie with fresh whipped cream, and my mom's lemon bars (which melted in your mouth). I try to make some of these dishes but there is no comparison from the original bakers.

## Getting Ready for Thanksgiving

When it comes to preparing for Thanksgiving, especially the large extravagant variety many Italian-Americans have, there is a lot to do. You must start with the basics: coordinating where it will be held, who will be there and at what time, what to serve, and who will bring and do what. Then there's the shopping, especially if it's going to take place at your home and/or you are the one preparing many, most, or all of the dishes. Luckily for my mom, my dad was very involved. He liked to cook and was easy to work with. In fact, they always pulled it off together, even when it was his birthday, which occasionally fell on Thanksgiving Day. In addition, my mom would always assign everyone a dish. I would bring the green bean casserole, my cousin Lana brought an appetizer (usually artichoke dip), Aunt Sherry brought a salad and a pie, my grandma came with stuffing and a dessert dish, Uncle Stevie brought the rolls, and so on. Plus, each person brought a bottle of wine.

Preparing the food is the next step and can take days. My parents often bought two enormous turkeys—one for serving and one for cutting up, putting into plastic bags, and sending home with all the guests. For days ahead, they were buying groceries and thawing turkeys. On Thanksgiving morning they were stuffing, butter brushing, cooking, and basting turkeys; boiling, mashing, and seasoning potatoes; as well as preparing yams, cranberries, and desserts.

Finally, you'll have to get the house ready by cleaning and decorating; buy or make a centerpiece; plan activities, special prayers, and toasts; set the table; and plan seating arrangements. Some things you might consider doing on Thanksgiving are making and exchanging Christmas lists; drawing gift-exchange names; telling what everyone is thankful for; watching family videos, slides, movies, or viewing photographs; and playing card games, board games, or boccie ball.

## Planning the Menu

If you will be serving turkey on Thanksgiving Day, you will need to purchase the right-size bird (or birds). This will depend on how many people will be attending the feast, how much they can eat, how many other dishes there will be, and the amount of leftovers you'd like to have. A common way to figure out how much turkey to buy is to figure one to one and a half pounds per person.

Unless you buy fresh, you'll most likely need to thaw the turkey, about one day for each four or five pounds, in the refrigerator. This doesn't include the day you will be cooking it. (The more time you give yourself, the better.) So, for a hard-frozen 20-pound turkey to be eaten on Thursday, you'll need to start thawing on the previous Saturday or Sunday.

Once the bird is thawed (and has no sign of ice in the body), remove its insides and neck. If you plan to stuff the turkey, use about ¾ cup of stuffing per pound, and insert lightly (just before cooking) in the neck and body cavity (as stuffing expands as it roasts). Tuck the drumsticks under the band of skin at the tail, or tie or skewer them to the tail.

Brush the turkey with butter or olive oil, tent with foil, and roast the bird, breast side up, in a 325-degree preheated oven. Take foil off for the last 45 minutes to allow the skin to brown. (Some people start with the foil off and finish with it on.) Turkey is done when the juice runs clear when you cut into the center of the thigh and the drumsticks can be removed easily. If you have a meat thermometer, insert it into the thigh, not touching the bone. It should register 180 degrees when done.

There are many different ways to cook turkeys; roasting is just one option. Consider barbecuing, smoking, and Crock-Pot cooking for small turkeys and turkey breasts. Plus, there are different ways to stuff a turkey, such as using quartered onions, celery, and carrots instead of bread stuffing. And there are alternatives to even having turkey—whole chickens, Cornish game hens, chicken breasts, duck, goose, quail, or even ground turkey in a meat sauce served over pasta.

There are also many options for side dishes. Stuffing, both in the turkey and cooked in a baking dish, varies greatly. Many Italian-Americans spruce up stuffing with Italian ingredients such as sausage, cheeses, nuts, vegetables, raisins, and spices. Other sides include potatoes—mashed, roasted, or in a casserole—and/or pasta dishes.

Lasagna is a common accompaniment to almost every holiday meal. Some families prepare the classic Italian lasagna with meat, sausage, and several cheeses, while others opt for a vegetable variety with the produce of the season. In addition, there are cranberries, cranberry sauce (homemade and canned), gravy (with and without giblets), corn, peas, green beans, yams, sweet potatoes, and any number of vegetable dishes, different kinds of casseroles, all types of salads, soups, and an array of desserts from pumpkin, apple, and rhubarb pies to Italian pastries and cookies.

Wine is also a big part of the Thanksgiving meal, and includes white, red, and sparkling varieties. One wine to try is Italian Moscato d'Asti from the Piedmont region. It is light, crisp, refreshing, and is great before and during the meal. Asti Spumanti, with its sweet and fruity taste, is also great. (See chapter 8 for more on wines.)

## Thanksgiving Recipes

Thanksgiving is a time of gratitude, prayer, and being with family. It's a time to cherish our blessings and strengthen our connections with the people in our lives. And Thanksgiving officially begins the holiday season, drawing us closer to the festivities of December.

## Antipasto Platter

Marinated mushrooms (about 1 pound mushrooms with stems off, soaked several hours in a mixture of: 1 cup lemon juice, 1 cup olive oil, ½ cup parsley, and 1 or 2 cloves of minced garlic)
Mozzarella cubes
Provolone cheese in cubes or sticks
Gorgonzola cheese slices
Rolled thin-cut meats (prosciutto or ham, turkey, salami, roast beef, capocollo)

Marinated artichoke hearts
Black olives
Green olives
Pepperoncini peppers
Tomato slices
Pimento
Other options include deviled eggs, eggplant, melon balls, anchovies, and pickles

Arrange items decoratively on platters and add garnishes of lettuce leaves, basil leaves, parsley, and lemon wedges. Create the following mixture—1 cup red wine vinegar, 4 cloves minced garlic, 1½ teaspoons oregano, and 1½ teaspoons basil—and drizzle over mozzarella cubes and vegetables as desired.

# Bruschetta

12 baguette slices
1 cup finely chopped Roma tomatoes
½ cup chopped red onion

2 tablespoons olive oil
1 teaspoon basil
Salt and pepper to taste

Arrange baguette slices on baking sheet and bake about 10 minutes at 425 degrees, or until lightly golden. Mix other ingredients together and spoon onto toasted baguette slices.

# Stuffed Mushrooms

2 cups bread crumbs
1 cup grated Parmesan cheese
2 cloves garlic, minced
1 tablespoon olive oil
1 tablespoon parsley

1 teaspoon basil
Salt and pepper to taste
12 large mushrooms, washed, stems removed

Mix bread crumbs, Parmesan cheese, garlic, olive oil, parsley, basil, salt, and pepper. Stuff mushrooms with mixture, place on cookie sheet, and bake at 325 degrees until hot and tender, about 15 minutes.

# Claro's Tortellini Salad

## Dressing

2 tablespoons lemon juice
1 tablespoon dijon mustard
2 cups olive oil
2 tablespoons white wine vinegar

2 teaspoons salt
2 teaspoons black pepper
2 cloves garlic

## Other

Package frozen cheese tortellini
2 cups frozen broccoli florets,
    thawed

1 red bell pepper, diced
½ cup toasted pignoli nuts

Make dressing for salad by whisking all dressing ingredients in bowl till creamy. Set aside. Follow package directions and cook tortellini till done. Drain pasta and put in large bowl. Add thawed broccoli and mix well. Add remaining ingredients and pour dressing over all. Mix and serve. Best if served at room temperature.

# Toni's Fried Eggplant

1 eggplant, sliced in ¼-inch slices
1 or 2 eggs, beaten
Seasoned bread crumbs
Olive oil
1 clove garlic, thinly sliced
2 large onions, sliced
2 large tomatoes, sliced in ¼-inch
    slices

12 ounces mozzarella cheese, sliced
    in ¼-inch slices
Parmesan or Romano cheese,
    grated
1 teaspoon garlic salt or powder
2 tablespoons parsley
¼ teaspoon pepper

Dip eggplant slices into egg and then into seasoned bread crumbs. In a skillet, heat olive oil and several garlic slices. Lightly brown eggplant on both sides. Place eggplant slices on a greased cookie sheet, and top each with slice each of onion, tomato, and mozzarella cheese. Sprinkle with grated Romano or Parmesan cheese, garlic salt, parsley, and pepper. Bake at 350 degrees for 15 to 20 minutes, or until cheese is melted and bubbling.

# Toni's Eggplant Parmesan

2 eggs
¼ cup milk
3 tablespoons olive oil
1 to 2 cloves garlic
2 eggplants sliced in ¼-to-½-inch
    slices

1 cup spaghetti sauce
½ pound sliced mozzarella cheese
2 white onions, sliced
½ cup Parmesan cheese
1 cup bread crumbs seasoned with
    salt, pepper, garlic, and parsley

Slightly beat 2 eggs together with milk in a small bowl. Heat olive oil and garlic in a skillet. Dip eggplant into egg mixture, then into bread crumbs. Place breaded eggplant in skillet and slowly brown both sides. Layer in a baking dish in this order: spaghetti sauce, browned eggplant, mozzarella, onion, Parmesan, and more spaghetti sauce. Repeat layers two times, ending with spaghetti sauce and Parmesan sprinkled on top. Bake covered at 350 degrees for 20 to 30 minutes. Remove cover and bake an additional 10 to 15 minutes, or until cheese is bubbling and lightly browned.

# Stuffed Green Peppers

1½ pounds ground beef
½ pound Italian sausage, casings
    removed
1 cup Italian seasoned bread
    crumbs
1 cup white rice, cooked
4 cans tomato soup

Parsley
Salt and pepper to taste
2 cloves garlic, minced
4 large green peppers, tops cut off,
    washed and drained
1 egg

Brown ground beef and sausage. Mix with bread crumbs, rice, 2 cans of tomato soup, egg, parsley, salt, pepper, and garlic. Fill peppers with mixture. Place remaining 2 cans tomato soup and three cans water in saucepan. Add stuffed peppers, tops up, cover, and simmer for 2 hours.

# LaVonne Marino's (Mimi's)
## Stuffed Artichokes

4 to 5 artichokes
3 cups spaghetti sauce, thinned
    with a little water
3 lemon slices

### For Stuffing

1 cup Italian bread crumbs
Small amount of minced garlic or
    garlic powder
Enough olive oil and tomato sauce
    to make mixture squishy
Black pepper

Wash and trim artichokes. Cut off about ½ inch from top. Trim tips of leaves. Cut off base. Hit artichoke on top of breadboard to open leaves.

Mix stuffing ingredients together by hand. Fill center of artichokes with stuffing, then pull leaves back and tuck stuffing inside. Stand artichokes upright in a saucepan; pour thinned spaghetti sauce over to almost cover; add 2 to 3 lemon slices, cover pan, and simmer over low heat for about 1 hour.

## Stuffed Onions

6 large onions, root cut off, peeled,
    and rinsed
3 tablespoons olive oil
¼ pound ground beef
2 cups bread crumbs
1 egg, beaten

1 tablespoon parsley
1 teaspoon basil
1 teaspoon salt
½ teaspoon pepper
¼ cup Parmesan cheese

Cut about a half inch off top of onions. Boil in salted water about 15 minutes (or until slightly tender). Drain and set aside. When cooled, scoop out the center of each onion and set aside. In a skillet, heat 2 tablespoons of the oil, add onion scoopings, and cook until tender. Add ground beef and cook until browned. In a large bowl, mix beef and onion pieces with bread crumbs, egg, basil, parsley, salt, and pepper. Fill onions with meat mixture and arrange in greased baking dish. Sprinkle Parmesan on top and then drizzle with 1 tablespoon olive oil. Bake at 350 degrees about 1 hour.

# Pepper-Stuffed Tomatoes

6 large (or 8 medium) tomatoes
2 tablespoons olive oil
3 bell peppers, cleaned, seeded, and chopped
1 white onion, chopped
2 cloves garlic, sliced

1 teaspoon basil
1 teaspoon parsley
1 teaspoon salt
½ teaspoon pepper
½ cup pine nuts
¼ cup Parmesan cheese

Cut tomatoes in half. Scoop out the pulp and set it aside. Place tomato halves on a serving platter. Heat oil in skillet and add peppers, onion, garlic, basil, parsley, salt, and pepper, and cook until peppers and onion are at desired tenderness. Add tomato pulp and stir about 2 minutes. Add pine nuts and mix for another 1 or 2 minutes, then remove from heat. When mixture is slightly cooled, scoop into tomato halves. Sprinkle with Parmesan if desired. Serve at room temperature or cooled.

# Pasta-Stuffed Peppers

2 tablespoons olive oil
1 onion, chopped
2 cloves garlic, minced
1 cup mushrooms, sliced
2 tomatoes, chopped
1 teaspoon basil

Salt and pepper to taste
½ package angel hair pasta, prepared and set aside
4 bell peppers, any color, cut in half lengthwise

Heat oil in skillet. Add onion, garlic, and mushrooms, and sauté until tender. Add tomatoes, basil, salt, and pepper, and mix together. Cook about 1 minute. Add pasta and mix well. Cook another 2 to 3 minutes. Fill pepper halves with the pasta mixture, and bake at 350 degrees until heated through (about 30 minutes).

# Tomato-Stuffed Peppers

4 bell peppers, cleaned, seeded, and cut in half lengthwise  
4 large tomatoes (or 6 Roma), chopped  
1 cup chopped onions  

2 cloves garlic, sliced  
1 tablespoon basil  
1 teaspoon salt  
½ teaspoon black pepper  
Parmesan cheese, to taste  

Preheat oven to 400 degrees. Place pepper halves in baking dish. Mix tomatoes, onions, garlic, basil, salt, and pepper in bowl. Spoon mixture into pepper halves and bake about 30 minutes, or until tender. Drizzle with oil. Sprinkle with Parmesan if desired.

# Claro's Stuffed Red Roasted Peppers

4 7-ounce roasted peppers  
1 cup seasoned bread crumbs  
3 cloves garlic, minced  
8 ounces Fontina cheese, cut in strips  
A few sprigs of fresh parsley, chopped fine  

¼ cup imported grated Romano cheese  
Salt and pepper  
Flour and beaten eggs (enough to dredge peppers in)  
Olive oil to fry peppers in  

Drain peppers and rinse with water. Open peppers, splitting one side so that they lay flat on the counter. Sprinkle with small amount of bread crumbs, reserving most for coating peppers. Add minced garlic, Fontina cheese, parsley, and grated Romano cheese. Roll up each pepper, keeping as much filling inside as possible, then dredge in flour, then egg, then seasoned bread crumbs, and set aside. Heat olive oil on medium-high heat in frypan. When the oil is ready, fry peppers till golden, turning once to brown evenly. Sprinkle with salt and pepper and serve. (A slice of ham or capocollo can also be rolled inside each pepper before frying.)

# Claro's Zucchini Fans

6 small fresh zucchini
2 ripe tomatoes, cored and sliced
½ cup seasoned bread crumbs
¾ cup grated Romano cheese
1 medium onion, sliced thin

1 tablespoon fresh garlic, minced
Salt and pepper to taste
2 tablespoons extra virgin olive oil
½ cup white wine

Preheat oven to 350 degrees. Wash zucchini and cut off stems and tips. Cut each zucchini into thin strips, being careful not to slice through at top (leave about ½ inch intact, and place in baking dish). Cut tomato slices in half again and place between sliced zucchini. Sprinkle tomato slices with bread crumbs and some of the grated cheese after placing them between zucchini. Sprinkle sliced onion on top of stuffed zucchini, along with remaining grated cheese. Top with garlic, salt, and pepper. Drizzle olive oil on top, then pour wine on bottom of baking dish. Bake for about 30 minutes, or until zucchini are cooked and the onions are slightly brown. The zucchini should still be firm. Can be eaten at room temperature. When serving, fan slightly on each plate and enjoy.

# Claro's Italian Sausage Stuffing for Turkey

2 pounds Italian sausage
½ cup butter or margarine
1 large onion, chopped
1 cup celery, diced
½ cup parsley, minced
2 4-ounce cans sliced mushrooms,
    drained

¾ cup pignoli nuts
6 cups cooked rice
Salt and pepper to taste
4 eggs

Remove sausages from casings and brown in a skillet, stirring and breaking apart while cooking. In separate pan, melt butter and sauté onions until golden. Add celery, parsley, mushrooms, and pignoli nuts. Cook a little more. Add rice, cooked sausage, salt, and pepper. Beat 4 eggs and stir into mixture. (This will stuff an 18-to-20-pound bird.)

# Garlic Mashed Potatoes

*(yields 8 to 12 servings)*

12 medium potatoes (about 4 pounds)
2 tablespoons olive oil
2 cloves garlic, minced
½ cup onion, chopped
1 cup milk

1 stick butter, at room temperature
¼ cup sour cream
1 tablespoon basil
1 teaspoon salt
½ teaspoon pepper

Wash and peel potatoes and cut into large pieces. Add 2 inches water to saucepan and bring to boil. Add potatoes and return to boil. Reduce heat and simmer for 20 minutes, or until potatoes are tender. While potatoes are boiling, heat oil in a skillet and add garlic and onion. Cook until soft and golden. Remove from heat and set aside. Drain potatoes and return them to the saucepan. Cook over low heat about 1 minute (to dry them). Place potatoes in a large bowl and mash with masher or mixer until lumps are gone. Gradually add milk. Mix until smooth and fluffy. Add butter, sour cream, garlic-and-onion mixture, basil, salt, and pepper, and mix thoroughly.

# Gina Schaffer's Traditional Tomato Sauce

1 cup olive oil
3 cloves garlic, diced
2 large (28-ounce) cans tomato puree
1 to 2 small (6-ounce) cans tomato paste (use 2 cans for thicker sauce)

Dried oregano
Onion powder
Fresh basil (about 5 good-size leaves)
Salt and pepper to taste

Simmer the oil and garlic until golden brown (preferably in a nonstick pot). Add the tomato puree and paste and stir until blended together. Keep heat low or the sauce will splatter. Add oregano—usually a thin layer that completely covers the surface of the sauce. Use about half the amount of onion powder. Roughly cut basil and add. Cover and simmer for about 30 to 45 minutes on low heat. Stir often to prevent sticking. Add salt and pepper to taste. (For thinner sauce, keep pot covered; for thicker sauce, keep pot uncovered.)

# Fettuccine Alfredo

1 pound fettuccine noodles
2 tablespoons olive oil
2 cloves garlic, minced
1 teaspoon basil

½ cup Parmesan cheese, grated
1 tablespoon butter
Salt and pepper to taste

Cook fettuccine noodles according to directions on the package. Drain and set aside. In a large skillet, heat oil and add garlic and basil. Add prepared noodles to the pan, along with the Parmesan cheese, butter, salt, and pepper. Mix well and heat through.

# Pesto Genovese

4 to 6 garlic cloves, chopped
16 large, fresh basil leaves
2 parsley sprigs
6 tablespoons Parmesan cheese,
    grated

¼ cup chopped pine nuts or walnuts
½ teaspoon salt
½ cup olive oil (do not substitute)
1 to 2 tablespoons butter
1 pound pasta, cooked and drained

In mortar and pestle, or in electric blender, crush or blend all ingredients except the oil to a smooth paste. Slowly blend in oil and stir until smooth. To serve with hot pasta, toss with 1 to 2 tablespoons butter, adding pesto to taste. Leftovers may be placed in a small jar, covered with olive oil, and refrigerated.

# Gina Schaffer's Meatballs

1 pound ground beef or turkey
    (If you use turkey, use 15 percent
    fat, not lean, which will make the
    meatballs too dry.)
1 egg
1 cup Italian bread crumbs

1 cup Parmesan cheese, grated
1 cup milk (with beef only, milk will
    make turkey too runny)
Fresh parsley
Salt and pepper to taste

Mix all ingredients together by hand, which makes the meat more tender. Roll into balls. Bake or pan fry to brown. If baking, bake at 350 degrees until brown, then slightly broil at the end. Add meatballs to your sauce and include the meat drippings for flavor.

# Gina Schaffer's Lasagna

| | |
|---|---|
| 1 box lasagna noodles | 1 egg |
| 1 pint Ricotta cheese | Parsley, chopped |
| 16 ounces Mozzarella cheese | Traditional Tomato Sauce (p.39) |

Cook lasagna noodles according to directions on the box. Drain and run under cold water to prevent them from sticking. Cut mozzarella in half; then cut one half into slices and the other into small cubes. In a large bowl, mix ricotta, mozzarella, egg, and parsley. Cover the bottom of a Pyrex baking dish with a layer of sauce, then place lasagna noodles until sauce is almost covered. With a tablespoon, scoop some of the cheese mix and dollop around on the noodles. Add another layer of noodles and cover with sauce. When you get to the top of the pan, take remaining mozzarella in slices and place on top so when melted the top will be covered with cheese. Cover with tinfoil and bake at 350 degrees for about 30 minutes. Remove foil and continue to bake another 15 minutes, or until the cheese is melted and the sauce is bubbly.

# The Italian Christmas Season

THE CHRISTMAS SEASON is the most festive and important time for Italian-Americans who carry out the traditions of their heritage. In addition to Christmas Eve and Christmas Day, which are huge celebrations filled with many Italian traditions, the season features several other opportunities for celebration.

Christmas is the most elaborately celebrated holiday in the Italian culture, with more special foods and practices than for any other occasion. Therefore, several chapters in this book are devoted to it. We will look at Christmas as it is celebrated in the United States by Italian-Americans—decorating and preparing the home, pre-Christmas parties and get-togethers, gifts and greetings, the Christmas Eve and Christmas Day celebrations of various families and individuals, and the foods.

But first, let's take a look at how Christmas and its related feast days are celebrated in Italy. While parts of the season are celebrated somewhat differently in Italy, many of our own traditions originated there.

In Italy the Christmas season begins with the feast of Santo Nicola (St. Nicholas) on December 6. This is followed by the Feast of the Immaculate Conception on December 8, the Feast of Santa Lucia (St. Lucy) on December 13, Christmas Eve on December 24, Christmas Day on December 25, and the feast of Santo Stefano (St. Stephen) on December 26. During this period of celebration, the religious season of Advent takes place, as does the Novena, a nine-day period of religious devotion before Christmas, during which time Catholics spend hours in preparation and prayer. (The number 9 represents the months Jesus was in the womb.) Then come the Italian twelve days of Christmas—from Christ's birthday to the feast of the Epiphany on January 6.

## Christmastime in Italy

Christmas in Italy is known as *Natale*, which means "birthday," and is an extremely festive time. Fairs, festivals, and parties take place throughout the month of December and early January. Streets are illuminated with Christmas lights and decorations everywhere. Cheery people smile, laugh, and wish each other well, and children are excited about the coming of Santo Babbo (St. Nicholas and/or Santa Claus) on December 24 and Befana on January 5 to bring them goodies.

Christmas in Italy is a highly religious occasion with church obligations and constant reminders of the true meaning of Christmas—to celebrate the birth of Christ—as well as celebrations of significant religious events and commemorations of saints. From December 6 through January 6, Italians devote a lot of time to prayer and church services.

The most distinguishing signs of Christmas in Italy are the abundant *presepio*, or manger scenes, featured throughout the cities. Also known as Nativity scenes or cribs, these elaborate creations of wood and plaster (and many other materials) can be seen on the lawns of churches, in the piazzas, and along the streets. They feature figurines of Mary, Joseph, baby Jesus, donkeys and oxen (said to have warmed the child with their breath), the three Wise Men and their gifts, angels, and a variety of props such as a shelter, crib, hay, and torches.

St. Francis of Assisi introduced the first Nativity scene in 1223 to clearly illustrate the story of Jesus's birth to his followers. He chose townspeople to play the various roles. Afterward, he performed mass in front of the Nativity scene. Since then, *presepi* of all kinds draw crowds all over Italy during the Christmas season. Many Italian families have a favorite

Nativity scene that they will go back and visit several times during the season.

Naples and Verona are known for their elaborate *presepi*, and making these scenes is a very popular local craft. Great scenes can also be found in Milan, Rome, and Sicily.

In Naples, the Nativity scenes are elaborate works of art that sometimes take months to assemble. They can be seen in front of houses and churches throughout the city, and may range in size from minute intricate designs (only an inch or two tall and wide) to massive displays with life-size figures with realistic characteristics, and extreme detail down to the facial expressions. Most scenes feature all the major characters (also called *pastori*), including the Holy Family, the Wise Men, shepherds, angels, and animals—as well as soldiers, musicians, and even Roman ruins. One elaborate scene features lavish costumes made of leather, silk, velvet, satin, and brocade, and features flying angels and a smoking *Vesuvius* (a volcano).

People bring enormous amounts of food to the displays—pasta dishes, pizzas, pork, sausages, egg dishes, cheeses, fruit, breads, and pastries—and leave them as an offering. People throw money at the *presepi* in the Galleria Umberto, which depicts lifelike Neapolitan scenes, to help pay for its upkeep. The Museo San Marino houses the largest collection of crêches in the world, including the oldest in existence: a life-size model made of wood dating back to the 1400s. At the Museo Nazionale di San Martino in Naples, an exhibit called "Il Presepe Cuciniello" features a collection of manger scenes dating back to the 1700s.

There is a festival in Naples on the narrow street called Via San Gregorio Armeno, which displays *presepi*. The street is covered with artisans selling Nativity scenes and figurines.

In Rome, a crêche is set up on the Spanish Steps and is a miniature version of an eighteenth-century street scene. A life-size Vatican's Manger in St. Peter's Square is set in front of a Christmas tree. There is a famous crêche with life-size figures in the Piazza San Retro, and another on the Trinità dei Monti stairway. A huge Christmas crêche exhibition called Cento Presepi ("One hundred Christmas cribs") is set up by the church of Santa Maria del Popolo. Some permanent *presepi* include a seventeenth-century Neapolitan scene with hundreds of figures at the main entrance to the Roman Forum.

In Milan, a large-scale Nativity scene can be found in the Mercato di Sant'Ambrogio.

*Presepi* in different parts of Italy range in materials. For example, in Sicily they are constructed from bone, ivory, coral, mother-of-pearl, and other sea materials. In Rome, they are made from more rural materials like pine and olive trees. In Naples, the city known for its artistic crèche scenes, they are made of everything from plaster to wood and even coral and gold.

In addition to the elaborate manger scenes on display in the towns, Italian families create their own Nativity scenes in their homes. Often called *presepios*, or crèches, these scenes are also full of detail and created with love. The tiny clay figures are sometimes called *santons*, or "little saints." It is traditional to move the little figures closer and closer to the manger each day until Christmas Eve, which is when the Baby Jesus is placed in the crib. During the Christmas season, Italian families pray in front of their Nativity scenes. Often, Italian families also add a miniature village to the scene, with little houses, shops, churches, fountains, and people.

Many families make their own *presepi* and all of the characters. However, there are several stores in which to purchase entire sets or individual parts. There is a store in Naples, along the narrow Via San Gregorio Armeno, called Pastori Artistici (meaning "artistic shepherds") that is entirely devoted to the figures used in the Nativity scene. The figures can also be bought at the annual Christmas fair in Piazza Navona.

## A Festive Time

In addition to the brilliant sights of the season, Christmastime in Italy offers magnificent sounds as well. Through the streets, carolers and musicians sing and play Christmas songs. Sometimes children will go caroling in their neighborhoods, earning coins for their performances.

Musicians, or *piferari*, playing flutes, oboes, bagpipes, and other instruments, parade through town, often in extravagant costumes from rustic mountain gear and sandals to bright red jackets and broad-brimmed hats with red tassels. In Rome and the Abruzzi region, musicians perform dressed in leather leggings under short bulky trousers that buckle under the knee, vests (that used to be made of sheepskin), velvet jackets, and pointed hats. Long ago, these *piferari* would walk over a hundred miles to town, playing music along the way for food and a place to rest.

Families in Italy decorate their homes for the Christmas season with sprigs of holly and mistletoe, lots of pine, candles, and Christmas trees adorned with fruits, candles, small wrapped gifts, chocolates, and ribbons. Many Italians have an artificial fir tree upon which they hang colored Christmas balls and lots of lights to symbolize the light Jesus shines on the world. Some decorations are made of needlework and other stitching, accented with ribbon and featuring images of Babbo Natale, wreaths, hearts, and candles. Many homes also feature Advent wreaths and Advent calendars. Stockings are often hung under the Christmas trees. Mistletoe is hung on doors as a sign of protection and good luck.

## Diverse Christmas Activities in Italy

A spectacular ceremony is held on Christmas Eve in Rome's Santa Maria Aracoeli church. The ramp is adorned with candles, costumed *piferari* play Christmas music, and at midnight the Baby Jesus is set in the crib (and left there until Epiphany, when another ceremony takes place). On Christmas Day at noon, the Pope gives his blessings to the crowd at Vatican Square.

Most Italian families also have a *ceppo*, a wooden pyramid-shaped frame—sometimes several feet high—decorated with colored paper, foil, linens, gilt pinecones, flowers, and little pennants. The tiers are adorned with candies, sweets, toys, small gifts, candles, fruits, ornaments, Christmas objects of all kinds, and on the bottom tier there is a Nativity scene.

Gift giving takes place throughout the Christmas season and varies from region to region. For example, it is common in some northern coastal areas to give gifts on St. Nicholas Day (December 6), while in Sicily, more gift giving takes place on St. Lucia Day (December 13). Throughout Italy, gifts are exchanged on Christmas Eve, Christmas Day, and Epiphany. Many spread the gift-giving ritual throughout the entire season.

# Advent

Advent, celebrated in Italy as well as by many Italian-Americans and Catholics around the world, is the religious season just before Christmas during which Christians prepare for the coming of Christ. Advent, which means "coming" or "arrival," is a time of preparation, waiting, and hope.

Advent begins on the fourth Sunday before Christmas and concludes on the Sunday closest. If Christmas Eve falls on a Sunday, it is counted as the fourth Advent Sunday. The purpose of Advent is to get ready for and celebrate Jesus' birth and God's presence in our lives, and to prepare for His final coming.

Advent possesses a penitential aspect in that Christians must prepare their souls for the second and final coming of the Lord. It also has a joyful component involving the celebration of the birth of the Baby Jesus in Bethlehem.

A common symbol for the Advent season is the Advent wreath, made up of four tall candles—usually three purple/lavender and one pink/rose—displayed on a circle, which is often adorned with greenery, evergreen branches, lights, and other decorations. Sometimes there is an additional (fifth) candle placed in the middle; this candle is white and represents Christ and his incarnation.

Everything about the Advent wreath is symbolic. The circle of the wreath is a reminder of God, His eternity, and His endless mercy that has no beginning or end. The greenery is a symbol of hope, renewal, and eternal life. The candles represent the light of God coming into the world through the birth of His son. The four outer candles stand for the period of waiting during the four Sundays of Advent.

The colors of the candles also mean different things. The purple candles represent the penitential spirit, humility, solemnity, and suffering, while the pink candle signifies the ultimate joy of Christ's birth. The flame symbolizes the celebration of light in the midst of darkness.

During the first week of Advent, one purple candle is lit. An additional candle is lit each week leading up to Christmas until finally all four candles burn. On the third Sunday, the pink candle is lit to symbolize the halfway point in the dark time of waiting. The third week of Advent is called *gaudete*, which is Latin for "joy." These candles are to remind Christians that the Lord will return to Earth, and the light of the candles grows brighter each week, signifying how much closer we are to Christmas.

On Christmas, the white center candle is lit, and from that point until Epiphany all five candles stay lit.

Each of the four weeks of Advent has a different theme that is the focus of meditation and the candle-lighting ritual. Week one is hope; two is peace; three is joy; and four is love.

During Advent masses, the celebrant and ministers use violet vestments—for the altar cloth and the celebrant's sash. Violet represents expectation, purification, and penance. On the third Sunday (*gaudete* Sunday) the vestments may be a richer shade of violet or rose. On Christmas Day, white is worn to represent joy and triumph.

The church is also often decorated with greenery—evergreen wreaths, boughs, and trees—that symbolizes the new and everlasting life brought through Jesus.

In Italy, many families bring Advent into their homes through Advent wreaths much like the ones found in churches. They also display Advent calendars, which are cards or posters with windows that can be opened, one each day of Advent, to reveal some symbol or picture associated with the Old Testament story leading up to the birth of Jesus.

## St. Nicholas Day

St. Nicholas Day is celebrated in Italy on December 6 in honor of San Nicola, the fourth-century saint who inspired our modern figure of Santa Claus and is the patron saint of Bari. On this day, the anniversary of his death, many Italian parents give small gifts to their children. It is a time to show generosity and selflessness. (An additional festival is held in his honor in the middle of May.)

St. Nicholas was known as "the Wonderworker," and many miracles are attributed to him. He was quiet and studious and spent much of his life behind the scenes doing God's work. He is recognized for his generosity, kindness, industriousness, and solicitousness.

Nicholas was born into a wealthy merchant family, and he used his wealth to help others. One story tells that he saved three sisters from poverty by giving them dowries so that they could find good husbands. The legend says that the sisters' father, a poor nobleman, couldn't raise the money for his daughters' dowries. Nicholas heard about this and tossed individual bags of gold for each girl into the house through the chimney. The third time, the nobleman saw Nicholas toss the bag of gold, which landed in a stocking hung over the fireplace to dry.

From then on, whenever people received an unexpected gift, they thanked Nicholas. Many Christmas traditions are rooted in this event, especially the legend of Old Saint Nick, or Santa Claus, who comes down the chimney on Christmas Eve and delivers gifts in stockings hung by the fireplace.

Another tale says that St. Nicholas restored to life three children who had been chopped up by a butcher and put in a brine tub.

He is known as the friend and protector of all those in trouble and is the patron saint of children, judges, charitable fraternities and guilds, travelers, murderers, pawnbrokers, thieves, merchants, paupers, scholars, sailors, bakers, travelers, maidens, and the poor.

St. Nicholas died of natural causes, and his remains were moved to Bari in 1087 and paraded triumphantly through the streets. His relics remain enshrined in the eleventh-century basilica of San Nicola, constructed in his honor, in Bari. Many European churches have been dedicated to him, and he has remained one of the most popular saints. In fact, many works of art and liturgical plays were based on his miracles.

## Immaculate Conception

The Feast of the Immaculate Conception, or Festa dell'Immacolata, is celebrated on December 8 to commemorate the Blessed Virgin Mary, mother of Jesus, and her freedom from original sin. This feast is a holy day of obligation, which means all Catholics are required to attend mass.

The observance of the Immaculate Conception began in the seventh century, and for many Italians it is the official beginning of Christmas.

In Rome, Christmas begins with the Feast of the Immaculate Conception, when the Pope visits the Piazza di Spagna (Spanish Square) and drapes garlands of flowers around the statue of the Madonna. Also called the Column of the Immaculate Conception, this sculpture—an ancient Roman column topped by a statue of Mary in honor of her Immaculate Conception—was designed by Luigi Poletti and put up in 1854. It was dedicated in 1857. After the Pope crowns the statue each year, many Catholics come forward and place flowers at the base of the column to pay their tribute.

At Torre del Greco in Naples, a major celebration takes place on Immaculate Conception. A huge triumphal float, with a statue of Mary on top, is carried by several townsmen through the streets. (This ceremony is also to commemorate the town's lucky escape from the 1861 eruption of Vesuvius; the rescue is attributed to Holy Mary.)

## Santa Lucia Day

On December 13, Italians celebrate the feast day of Santa Lucia, or St. Lucy, the Queen of Light. On this day, people in Italy refrain from eating bread or anything with wheat flour in it. In Sicily, pasta is replaced by *panelli*, potatoes, and rice (in the form of *arancine*, golden croquettes shaped and fried to the color orange and filled with chopped meats). Some Sicilians eat *cuccia*, a dessert made of whole-wheat berries, sweetened ricotta, candied orange, and shavings of chocolate.

Saint Lucia is a fourth-century Italian saint who carried food to the Christians hiding in the tunnels below Sicily. She wore candles on her head to light her way. She was from a wealthy family, but chose to devote her life to giving her money to the poor. She was killed by the Roman government for her religious convictions.

St. Lucia is the patron saint of virgins and the blind. On her feast day, a young girl dresses in a white gown with a red sash, and puts an evergreen wreath with five or more lighted candles on her head. She brings coffee and rolls to family members in their bedrooms before the light of dawn.

## Saturnalia

Celebrating the holidays in Italy has its roots in two strong traditions—Christian/Catholic (the birth of Christ) and the ancient Roman pagan rituals. One such pagan tradition is known as Saturnalia, which is an ancient Roman celebration that takes place on December 17.

Saturnalia, a winter solstice ritual, began as feast days for Saturn, the god of agriculture and sowing as well as the Roman god of kings, and Ops, the goddess of plenty. Winter solstice is the point when the sun is at its lowest and weakest. This is considered the turning point of the year, when the light will begin to grow stronger and brighter. The Romans called it *Dies Natalis Invicti Solis*, "the Birthday of the Unconquered Sun [or the Invincible Sun]."

Winter solstice, also known as Yule, celebrates the birth of the new solar year and the beginning of winter. It celebrates light, the rebirth of the sun, and the continuity of nature's cycles. Ancient cultures were afraid the sun would never return, so they engaged in ceremonies to bring it back.

In Italy, Saturnalia is a week-long feast of "total reversal" from December 17 through December 23 or 24. Businesses and schools close, misunderstandings are forgotten, and fighting is stopped. Celebrations include masquerades, huge feasts, festivals and fairs, gift giving, relaxation, time spent with loved ones, prayers for protection of winter crops, and religious observance. Another tradition in Italy used to be choosing a mock king, also known as the Lord of Misrule—or the Bean King, because he was chosen via bean ballot. This custom has evolved into the holiday tradition of baking a cake with a bean inside, traditionally on Epiphany, and called Twelfth Day Cake.

In Rome, the Saturnalia festival included decorating the home with greenery and lighting candles and lamps to chase away the spirits of darkness. In fact, many Christmas traditions are said to have grown from the Saturnalia/winter solstice traditions—the Yule log, evergreens, and mistletoe.

These days Christmas (the birth of Christ) and Saturnalia (the birth of Unconquered Sun) are generally combined and celebrated mainly on December 25. However, some still commemorate separately Saturnalia on December 17.

## Christmas Eve and Christmas Day

On Christmas Eve, *la vigilia*, Italian families light candles throughout their homes, gather around their *presepios*, and pray. The children take turns telling the story of Christmas and the birth of the Holy Bambino. In Rome, cannon shots fired from the Castle San Angelo at sunset on Christmas Eve proclaim the start of the night's holy observance. A twenty-four-hour fast ends with an elaborate Christmas feast.

December 24 is a day of abstinence from meat, but the evening meal is still usually a lavish banquet. After a day of fasting, dinner is often served at seven or eight P.M. Because of the church penitential rule of *mangiare di magro*, which means everyone eats fish on holiday eves to purify the body and get it ready for the big feasts that follow, the Christmas Eve dinner consists mostly of fish.

The menu can include *capitone* (especially in Venice, Rome, and Naples), a dish made with fried eels, baccala (salted cod), and any number of seafood dishes—shrimp, squid, octopus, or smelts—ranging from region to region. A traditional vegetable dish is *cardoni*, of which Jerusalem artichokes and eggs are the chief ingredients. *Frittos mistos* (vegetables dipped in batter and deep-fried) are also popular. Sweets include *torrone*, a nougat candy, and cannoli, or pastries filled with cream cheese. Panforte of Siena is an elaborate and tasty confection from Tuscany.

Most Italian families attend midnight mass, after which they return home to open gifts. The youngest child in the family will place the Baby

Jesus (the Bambino) in the manger. Many families have a large crock, called the Urn of Fate, in which presents have been placed and from which they are now drawn.

In Italy, Santa Claus is called Babbo Natale (Father Christmas) and may bring small gifts at Christmas.

On Christmas Day a huge feast is served. It often includes a turkey or ham and side dishes of pasta, vegetables, and lentils. It is often followed by espresso and dried fruits. Of course, the meal varies from region to region. In Trentino, it is customary to have a Christmas apple pie. People in Venice might eat a clam-based soup, prosciutto-and-fontina-stuffed chicken with broccoli, and *torte di mele*. North of Rome, several varieties of ravioli are served as side dishes. In Sicily, *cassata* is the popular choice for dessert.

Children sometimes write letters to their parents asking for forgiveness for the wrongs they have done in the prior year and promising to be better in the year to come. They hide these notes under their father's dinner plate, and he later finds the notes and reads them out loud.

A major part of the Christmas Eve and Christmas Day celebrations in Italy revolves around the feasting on traditional foods. We will explore this element in depth in chapter 7, as many of the food traditions carry over from Italians in Italy to Italian-Americans, more so than any other traditions.

After dinner, many Italian families gather around the table to play Tombola, the Italian version of Bingo.

## St. Stephen's Day

The Feast of St. Stephen, Santo Stefano, is celebrated in Italy on December 26, which is known as Boxing Day in some other European countries. In Italy, it is a day for visiting friends.

St. Stephen, known as one of the first "social workers" in the Church, devoted his life to feeding the poor. His feast was assigned to the day after Christmas because he holds a unique place among all the saints of the New Testament: he was the first martyr for Christ and was stoned to death while praying for his enemies in God's name.

He was venerated as the patron saint of horses, which in pre-Christian times were sacrificed at the winter solstice. The period between Christmas and Epiphany was a time of rest for domestic animals, specifically horses, the most useful servants of man. In some places, horses are still blessed in front of the church on St. Stephen's Day.

Popular foods to serve on this day are St. Stephen's Horns, bread in the form of a horseshoe, and roast suckling pig.

## New Year's Eve/St. Sylvester's Night

In Italy, December 31 not only marks New Year's Eve, but it is also the feast of St. Sylvester, known as Feste Nazionali Capodanno, or San Silvestro. The nighttime celebration includes fireworks and a "good luck" dinner that typically consists of *cotechino e lenticchie*, steamed sausages and lentils. Plus, wearing any piece of red clothing is also supposed to bring luck.

Saint Sylvester was a priest who was born in Rome. He acted as counselor and spiritual director of Constantine, and is often shown in various scenes with the emperor. He died before Constantine and was buried on December 31, 335.

Saint Sylvester took pleasure in giving hospitality to Christians passing through Rome. He would take them with him and wash their feet, serve them at his table, and give them his charity in the name of Christ.

While the principal scene represented is that of the baptism of Constantine, St. Sylvester is also shown trampling a dragon, with a chained dragon or bull and a tiara, with an angel holding a cross and olive branch (the peace of the Church), or with St. Romana. He is considered the patron saint of high persons in delicate situations. He was considered a great pope, and today is especially venerated in Pisa.

On New Year's Eve, fireworks explode to welcome the new year. Many people throw old unwanted things out the window in the hope of forgetting the bad things that happened during the last year and to ensure good luck and fortune in the new one. At midnight, everyone toasts with a glass of Italian sparkling wine.

On New Year's Day, many Italians have a feast that includes lentils, symbolizing money, and *zampone*, the fatty pig's foot, which is a symbol of abundance. An ancient Roman New Year's Day tradition was to give family and friends branches of greenery for good luck.

## The Celebration of Epiphany

Epiphany, or Epifania, is celebrated in Italy on January 6, the eve of which (January 5) is the twelfth night, or Little Christmas. Epiphany, which means "revelation," celebrates the day the Wise Men reached Bethlehem— the day of the revelation of Jesus' birth.

The famous carol "The Twelve Days of Christmas" was written about the days between December 25 and January 6. In Italy, Epiphany is the last day of the Christmas season, when the main exchange of gifts takes place.

In many cities in Italy, a traditional Epiphany procession moves through the streets, leading to a Nativity scene. In addition, many Italian families bless their homes with holy water and incense. The water prepared on the eve of Epiphany is used to ward off evil spirits and purify the home and family. In Rome, a toy and sweet fair takes place featuring a procession, led by La Befana, to the fountains of Piazza Navona. In Milan, a procession of the Rei Magi ("Three Kings") takes place. And in some places, on the evening of January 5, children wear masks or costumes and go door to door for treats (similar to our Halloween).

## The Legend of La Befana

On the night before Epiphany, children hang stockings on the fireplace or leave their shoes by the doorway for the kindly old witch Befana, or La Befana, to fill with gifts. Children will often write notes or wish lists and hide them up the chimney for La Befana to find. If the children are good, La Befana fills the stockings or shoes with candies, nuts, fruits, and little toys; and if they're bad, a lump of coal. In Italy today, some candy shops sell *carbone*, which is black rock candy that looks like pieces of coal. Sometimes it is left in children's stockings along with other goodies for fun.

The legend is that La Befana was invited by the three Wise Men to join them in their quest for the Baby Jesus. However, she was so busy with housework she delayed her journey. She was never able to catch up with them and locate them, and therefore missed out on the chance to bring gifts to the Christ Child. She frantically ran around looking for them while carrying gifts for Jesus, still holding on to the broom she was using to clean her house. Magically, she began to fly on her broom, but she never found the Wise Men or the child. It is said that to this day, on the evening before Epiphany, La Befana wanders in search of the Holy Child, visiting each home in the hope of finding Him inside. Instead she leaves gifts for other children.

La Befana is depicted as a woman on a flying broom, and is often old and ugly—but the children of Italy love her anyway.

In Rome, in Piazza Navona, there is a typical toy and sweet market. Here, the La Befana herself will give you some sweets.

On Epiphany, there are many street processions in which a masked La Befana and a band of followers make their way down the street. Many people place Befana dolls in their windows, welcoming her to their homes. At the end of the celebration the Befana dolls are sometimes burned to symbolize eliminating the bad things of the old year to make room for good things in the new year.

Many parties take place on Epiphany in Italian homes. It is a time to visit friends and relatives, and people might spend the day either entertaining guests who come to visit or out and about visiting others. La Befana's function is that of reaffirming the bond between people.

# More Italian Christmas Season Traditions and Staples

**Christmas candles/tapers** are lit in many Italian households at Christmastime. Long ago, Christians lit a large candle on Christmas Eve, which symbolized Christ as the light of the world, and left it illuminating the Nativity all night long.

**The burning of the Yule log** is another Christmas tradition that takes place in Italy. Many families will gather an oak log from nearby woods and burn it in the fireplace from Christmas to New Year's Day.

A product of the blending of Christian and pagan beliefs, this ritual represents the vitality of fire, and its powerful and purifying effects. It is believed that the burning of the log eliminates the old year and all of its evils. An old Christian belief about the Yule log is that while families are away at Midnight Mass on Christmas Eve, the Virgin Mary brings her newborn baby into the house and warms him by the fire.

The oak of the Yule log symbolizes the new solar year, good luck, and strength.

**Evergreens** symbolize rebirth and life amid winter whiteness, and are used to decorate doors, windows, and fireplaces. The prickliness of the evergreens is believed to ward off or snag and capture evil spirits who try to bring harm to the family.

**Holly** represents good luck and was used by the ancient Romans in their winter celebrations. They used to hang it over doorways to invite good spirits to bless their homes.

*5*

# Italian-American Christmas

WHILE MANY OF THE CHRISTMAS season traditions that take place in Italy carry over to Italian-Americans living in the United States, there are some variations. Several holiday practices have been replaced by or simply blended in with the American way of life.

For example, few Italian-Americans celebrate Santa Lucia Day and Epiphany in the same way they are celebrated in Italy. However, many Catholic Italian-Americans attend mass on holy days—Immaculate Conception, Christmas Day, and Epiphany. They also participate in Advent practices. For Italian-American children, the majority of the focus is on Christmas Eve and Christmas Day. Santa Claus is the main gift bearer, not La Befana.

The most significant aspect of the Italian-American Christmas season is spending time with family, feasting, and celebrating. Everyone is included in the celebrations and is expected to be there. The atmosphere is usually casual, and everyone feels welcome and at ease. The young and old sit together, talking, laughing, eating, and drinking.

There are numerous parties and get-togethers throughout the season. Homes are open to visitors and filled with festive foods, baked goods, and cocktails. People come together. Music is played. Carols are sung. Memories are made.

The Christmas season is filled with much to do from pre-Christmas planning and preparing to executing enormous feasts. Italian-Americans tend to do a lot of entertaining, visiting, and getting together with family and friends during this time. Shopping, cooking, and eating are also popular activities.

Many Italian-American homes are festively decorated with Christmas trees, lights, Nativity scenes, and all sorts of decorations. Stockings are hung on mantels. Homes are filled with delicious aromas of pine, scented candles, baked goods, and sauces.

Children prepare lists for Santa Claus, with whom they have their pictures taken at shopping centers prior to Christmas. On Christmas Eve, they leave Santa milk and cookies to enjoy as he puts goodies under the tree and in their stockings.

## Christmas Eve Activities

For many Italian-Americans, Christmas Eve is the major celebration, while for others it is Christmas Day. Some treat both equally. For the Italian-American, Christmas Eve features a big family gathering with a huge feast, usually consisting of fish and seafood courses (many Italian-Americans don't eat meat on Christmas Eve). The fish dinner often consists of seven, ten, or twelve courses of fish, plus pastas, breads, and desserts. Some popular Christmas Eve dinners include *baccala*, *capitone* (eel), squid, smelt, octopus, clams, shrimp, lasagna, and spaghetti. (Note: It is said that a seven-fish-course dinner represents the seven sacraments or gifts of the Holy Ghost.)

After dinner, some families play games such as cards and Tombola, roast chestnuts, and retell the story of Christmas and the birth of Jesus. The evening is often concluded by attending Midnight Mass and then coming home and opening presents.

# Christmas Day Activities

Italian-American Christmas Day celebrations often include another huge meal, usually an afternoon dinner consisting of anything from veal cutlets and lasagna to roasted chicken and potatoes to turkey and stuffing and all the trimmings. Many families attend mass on Christmas morning instead of Christmas Eve, and many also open gifts on this day as well.

# Christmas Memories

The following section contains warm Christmas memories from an assortment of Italian-Americans.

### My Mother

When my mom, Toni, was growing up in Ohio, her first-generation Italian-American relatives celebrated Christmases as traditionally as possible. She remembers her grandparents, Nicholas and Josephine Marino, living just down the street. Her aunts, uncles, and cousins all lived in the same vicinity as well. Nicholas's and Josephine's house was the central holiday gathering place. Later celebrations were held at Aunt Dana's house.

Mom says: "Two days before Christmas, my dad would go out and buy the squid. The kids would help him and my uncle Sammy to clean it. Uncle Sam would say, 'Want to pop a few eyeballs?' I remember we had to pull out the backbone, remove the skin, turn it inside out, and remove the guts, clean the tentacles, and snap the mouth. When the men and the kids were finished cleaning it, the women would sit at the kitchen table and stuff it with a bread crumb dressing, and then sew the end of each one to hold in the stuffing and then cook it in sauce.

"On Christmas Eve, we would have the squid with spaghetti and salad with endive, and for dessert *scartis* (a fried dessert with honey and nuts), cannoli, and rum balls. After dinner, the men would play poker. As kids we would sit on their laps and count the money—they played with chips and real money. We'd stack it and make it all pretty. They would tell us how much to put in, and everything was great until they started losing and they would say 'Get the hell out of here. . . .' Meanwhile, the women would drink coffee and gossip. When it was time to go, the men would go out and start the cars. The moms and kids would then go out to a warm car, go home, and get ready for Christmas morning. On Christmas Day, we would open gifts and then go back to the relatives' for another feast—sometimes it was sweet potatoes and roasted chicken—and more dessert."

## My Own Christmas Memories

Once my mom and her family moved to California, along with all the other relatives, the Christmas Eve celebrations took place in a rented hall. The hall is where my own Christmas memories begin.

The Christmas season meant baking all kinds of cookies, especially sugar cookies in various shapes—Santas, reindeer, snowmen, stars, ornaments, angels—that we would paint with frosting. It was about making little tree ornaments out of clothespins, felt, and paint, and playing my parents' old Christmas records—Bing Crosby, Brenda Lee, the Beach Boys, Elvis, and Frank Sinatra—on the stereo. It meant going shopping for the perfect tree, deciding whether to have it flocked or not, decorating that tree, and taking turns with my brother each year being the one Dad would lift up to put the star on top. There were also visits to Santa, holiday dance recitals, school programs, and church plays. There were the TV specials like *Rudolph the Red-nosed Reindeer*, *Frosty the Snowman*, *A Year Without Santa Claus*, and *The Grinch who Stole Christmas*, and trips through Toys "R" Us, pointing out to our parents the things we wanted, finding the right Christmas pajamas to wear on Christmas Eve, and looking for the perfect dress for church on Christmas Day.

And then came Christmas Eve. That was when the Americanized traditions were set aside and the Italian ones kicked in. On Christmas Eve we went to the hall. It was a big recreation room at a local park, and twenty-plus relatives gathered there. There were the young, old, very old, and the kids. There was music, both recorded and live—Uncle Tony and his accordion. There was food—every kind of pasta dish you can imagine, as well as breads, cakes, cookies, pastries, and of course, stuffed squid. Everyone would talk, laugh, eat, drink. The grown-ups played cards. The kids ran around and played. At some point, Santa would visit and hand out gifts to all the kids.

As I got older, the hall tradition faded out. Instead, Christmas Eves took place at my grandparents' house. The squid tradition carried on. I remember my mom and my grandpa being in charge of going out and buying the squid two days before Christmas and cleaning it, then handing it over to my grandma, who would stuff it with the bread crumb stuffing and sew it up and cook it in sauce. On Christmas Eve it was served with spaghetti, and there would always be a separate squidless sauce for those of us who thought squid was pretty gross. Prior to Christmas Eve dinner there would be an entire pre-meal—antipasto, chicken wings, pizza, and so on. Served with dinner would be some sort of chicken, Italian sausage (we didn't follow the no-meat tradition), peppers, salad, eggplant, and bread. For dessert, we would have pies, cookies, cannoli, petit fours in Christmas colors, and coffee. After dinner and helping with dishes, we had our mini gift exchange with our grandparents, aunt, uncle, and cousins.

The memories of Christmas Eves at the hall are so vivid that I hardly remember the festivities of Christmas morning, when my immediate family did our gift opening, which was an elaborate procedure. As very young kids, my brother and I would be so excited we would wake up as early as five A.M., sit around talking about what surprises might be in store for us, and after an agonizing wait, try waking our parents at five thirty, only to be told to go back to bed for another hour or so. After our parents got up and put their robes on, got coffee made, and took out the camera, we could enter the living room, where we each could open one gift at a time—making it last and letting everyone see what the others got. Then my dad would make us a big breakfast—eggs, bacon, hash browns, toast—after which we got dressed and went to church. Later, the other relatives would come over for the Christmas Day feast—turkey, mashed potatoes, gravy, stuffing, cranberries, yams, salad, and bread, followed by pies, pastries, cookies, and coffee. Throughout the evening, other friends and relatives would stop by to visit and share in dessert and coffee.

## Diane Reid

My husband's cousin remembers her Christmases with her grandparents. "Christmas memories were always with Nanny and Parter, and always around the kitchen," says Diane. "Always about the favorite Christmas cookies and food. Nanny made a fried cookie—like pizza dough covered with cinnamon and sugar—on Christmas Eve. I couldn't wait to eat one. I remember the way Parter wrapped gifts with elaborate bows and Nanny's envelopes with cash for gifts. She always kept them in her apron pocket and was so excited to give them out. The best part was holding hands in a very large circle to say grace. Dinner was always Nanny's lasagna. Nanny sang songs in Italian she knew as a child. Parter would put on Italian music and Frank Sinatra and we'd all sing along. We celebrate in smaller groups now."

## Josie Vinci and Dorothy Pantleo

Josie and Dorothy are longtime friends who first met at the age of seven when they lived in Lincoln Heights, a onetime almost-all-Italian neighborhood in Los Angeles. They both grew up with parents who were born in Italy and practiced many Italian traditions. They ended up marrying Italian men, raising families, and holding on to many of the traditions of their heritage. Both say their homes are where the families congregate.

Josie's parents came from Piana de Albanesi, near Palermo (all her sisters were born there; she was the only one born here). "These days, on Christmas Eve we go to mass around four P.M. and then come home and eat and have presents," says Josie. "But when I was a kid, we didn't dare open presents before Midnight Mass. We'd have fig cookies and a fish dinner. Our Christmas Day is more Americanized—prime rib and a pasta (lasagna, stuffed shells, or manicotti). We used to have veal cutlets. We also have green olives, which I crack, mix equal parts olive oil and balsamic vinegar, garlic, carrots, and celery and marinate. We also always had black olives, stuffed artichokes, shrimp, pasta (like a baked ziti), and cannolis."

Both Dorothy's parents were from Sicily. According to Dorothy, "Christmas Eve is the big celebration in my family. We always have *bac-*

*cala*, all kinds of vegetables, frittatas, stuffed artichokes. We don't do anything special on Christmas Day except have another big feast—prime rib and the usual things that go with it. We also have *sfinges*, cannolis, and the men play bocci."

## David Manzari

David is a college student at UCLA and a part-time waiter at a restaurant called Bella Italia. He moved here from Bari with his parents and two brothers seven years ago and recently became a U.S. citizen. He says that while some of the traditions his family celebrated in Italy have been dropped, many are still practiced.

"Christmas is the same here as in Italy," says David. "We put up the tree, decorate it, decorate the whole house, and put up a Nativity scene. On December 24, we gather around the table for a big dinner that my mom cooks. At midnight we open presents. In Italy we would go around the house and bless every room with prayers and songs such as 'Ave Maria' and 'Padre Nostro.' The youngest kid in the family, which was me, would carry the Baby Jesus around. Now we just say a prayer.

"For Christmas Eve fish dinner, the first course is risotto with salmon, then *sgombro* (a fishlike eel, marinated and greasy). For appetizers we have calamari and more. In Italy we would have raw fish and mussels. We also have a flat dough pastry with anchovies inside, called *sfogliaea*, which is cooked crispy and crunchy.

"On December 25, we have a big lunch or brunch, which is a long meal. In Italy it included the whole family, but now it's just the five of us. We have meat, broth, homemade pasta, and turkey or chicken (boiled). Every city/region has its own style of cooking.

"Epiphany is not celebrated here. In Italy, we would hang stockings on the fireplace and also receive gifts for that. Befana, a witch with a broom, brings candy if you were good, or coal, which is sweet and edible, if you were bad. Another fairy tale was if you woke up during the night and tried to look for her you got beat with her broom—kids were scared."

## Sederina "Rina" Mele

Rina owns and runs the Bella Italia restaurant along with her husband, Franco, and their sons, Pino and Michael. They moved to the United States from Bari twenty-eight years ago. Rina says: "During the Christmas preseason I shop with family and do lots of Italian baking. Everyone gets together to put out decorations. Franco puts the lights on the house. On San Nicola Dibari (St. Nicholas Day), the family rents a boat and goes onto the water with a big feast and music. On Immaculate Conception we attend a mass only. Starting on St. Lucia Day, we pray for twelve days in front of Nativity scenes to the St. Joseph and Santa Maria, before Jesus is born.

"On Christmas Eve morning we fry the *vinilé*, which are doughnuts we dip in sugar, and have them with espresso. Later that day, we have a fish dinner with many courses. First we eat *rappinni* with lemon and anchovies; second, spaghetti with sauce; next, eel, fish, muscles, clams, lobster, and baccala. We eat together as a family and then go to Midnight Mass.

"On Christmas Day, we wake up, open presents, and take pictures. The family comes by to wish us a Merry Christmas. Our meal consists of several courses: antipasto; the wedding soup; lasagna; meat with sauce; lamb; fried vegetables; roasted chestnuts; espresso; Italian cookies; and panettone. Afterward, more friends come by and we play Tombola. On the day after Christmas, which is St. Stephen's Day, we eat turkey soup."

## Tery Spataro

Tery lives in New York but was born and raised in Connecticut. Her mom's family is from Naples, and her dad is Calabrian. While it's hard for the family to get together for the holidays with everyone so spread out, her fondest memories are those of the traditional Italian Christmases of the past.

Tery remembers: "Everyone would gather at my grandparents'—on my mom's side—house. It was the center. My family is spread out now, but we used to spend the night before at my grandmother's house. They did the fish dinner—fried smelt, trout, and so on. I'm not the cook in the family. The entire family was there—twenty to thirty people. Downstairs there were rows and rows of tables. We always had lasagna with ten layers, and went to Midnight Mass.

"Christmas Day was also spent at my grandmother's house. I remember her running around the house pulling everything together. There was an enormous tree and all the cousins came. What is most memorable was how warm it felt and how good the house smelled. There was always sauce cooking. There was a turkey and lots of salads, including an antipasto salad. They would be shopping for days, going to two or three Italian markets, where I remember there being sawdust on the floor and smelling the various cheeses.

"The Nativity scene was a big deal. My dad, a carpenter, made the wood part of the Nativity scene, and we went out and bought the rest. My mom has always been big on the decorating, and still decorates the whole house. There are reindeer and a sled you could sit in that my grandfather, also a carpenter, made. I also remember the Christmas cookies. The women in the family got together and cooked for days and days. I miss the big holiday celebrations and having all those people around."

## Joyce Spataro

Joyce, who lives in Arizona, is Tery's mother. She says: "We always had a Christmas tree and always a Nativity set. On Christmas Day, my dad would visit all the neighbors to wish them a Merry Christmas, and one of us would always go with him. We always opened our gifts on Christmas morning, never Christmas Eve. We always got together with our grandparents, aunts, uncles, and cousins on Christmas Day.

"For Christmas Eve dinner, my mother always made six different kinds of seafood: cod, smelts, eel, sole, shrimp, and flounder. She also made macaroni with an anchovy-and-garlic sauce. We never had meat on Christmas Eve. Also with this meal was a salad that had several types of olives, celery, peppers, tomatoes, and more. After the meal there was coffee and anisette for the adults, as well as homemade cookies and either a rum cake or fruitcake. The children usually had cookies or ice cream.

"Christmas Day dinner always started with either soup or antipasto. For the main meal, there was always pasta, such as lasagna, ravioli, cavatelli, or manicotti, with a red sauce that had meatballs, sausage, and braciole. There was always a roast—beef or pork—or a stuffed chicken and assorted vegetables. Every holiday my mother put a large bowl of mixed fruit and a bowl of mixed nuts on the table. This was there before and after the meals. Coffee and espresso were always served after the meal, along with a tray of cookies and cakes. We always had an Italian candy called Torrone, which was a wafer nougat candy. We made several types of cookies, including cherry delights, butter balls, rum balls, pignoli almond cookies, macaroons, honey cookies, and anise cookies.

"One year the family made a Santa sleigh with reindeer. You could sit in the sleigh, and every year we would get together at my parents' home and put the sleigh out on the lawn. It was all lit up. When we had children they would all sit in the sleigh."

## Ginny (Granieri) Craven

My husband's aunt, Ginny, says, "As a child from a traditional Italian family, what stands out most to me is that there was always plenty of food throughout the holidays. There were lots of homemade cookies and breads. Both my mom and my grandmother—we called her 'Nanny'—were excellent in the kitchen, so the variety was incredible. The holidays always seemed to bring everyone together. Family and friends filtered in and out of our house constantly. In due time, it was all around that there were always goodies at the Granieris'! You would never come to our house for a meal or snack and leave hungry . . . that's for sure. As soon as your plate was empty, Mom or Nanny would be sure you had seconds!

"The house was always decorated accordingly. For Christmas, there were always lots of decorations, which included wreaths, holly, candles, lights, and a fully decorated Christmas tree surrounded by loads of presents. Christmas music played a few weeks prior and mixed with the smells of fresh-baked bread or whatever was in the oven. It made for a very enjoyable and tasty celebration.

"Christmas is quite different now that my mom and nanny have passed away. The traditional aspects have diminished. I have tried to preserve as many as I can, but unfortunately, they are few. But with my memories of being a child, I plan to rejuvenate more traditions and put them into play for the future. Christmas is quiet now, since family does not gather like we used to. Everyone is spread out all over and we all have busy lives, so it has hindered our family gatherings. I very much get into the Christmas season and look forward to all the same decorations and enjoy baking. I try to keep the smells of Christmas alive!"

## Michael Granieri

Michael, my husband's cousin, says, "My memories of Christmas as a child in particular were very, very happy. Big families, big food, big Christmas. I particularly remember Christmases with my grandma and grandpa (that of course meant Nanny, too) in Santa Barbara. Grandma gracefully had pastries, mixed nuts, coffee cake, cheese and crackers, and just the right drink on every coffee table. Grandma made it look effortless, even though she worked for days, even weeks, preparing the perfect family Christmas. Grandma would line us cousins up on the same couch, regardless of how many of us were there and how old we were becoming, because she always wanted to have a picture of her grandchildren. This might have been her reward for her labor. Grandpa was always smiling and talking about school and grades and other stuff. Nanny just glowed. Nanny was the best! She must have kissed me a thousand times and made me feel like I was the only person in the world when she spoke to me.

"My mom and aunts always pitched in in the kitchen and brought dishes to complement Grandma's good work. I particularly remember my mom stressing out about making sure that her contribution was perfect and that her dish would blend in with the rest of the entrees on the dining room table.

"My family has scattered since Grandma's death. Today, I have a family, a perfect wife, a son after his father, and a beautiful yellow lab named Chase. My sister also has a family the same size as mine, and a dog. Because of that, holidays are touch and go—sometimes together, sometime not. I like it that way. Regardless of where we go—my wife's family is scattered in five different states—the food is always good."

## Mary Fanara

Mary is the owner of Fanara's Italian Restaurant in Duarte, California. She was born in Sicily and moved here with her parents when she was seven. She says, "All the holidays revolved around religion and revolved a lot around family. Christmas and Easter are the biggest. Many people would go to church all day and then spend the evening having huge amounts of food. On the religious holidays in Italy there were processions—someone would carry the Baby Jesus, people would dress up. My parents used to go to church for hours; they loved to go and they felt good about it. We didn't get into the Christmas tree and decorations. It was more about church.

"A lot of baking took place at the holidays. The little town where we lived had large community ovens, wood-burning ovens, which were a big deal. The women would mix up their dough at home and then go to these ovens to bake large amounts of bread.

"On Christmas Eve, we used to do the fish dinner. We had *baccala*, the dried fish, which my mother would soak for days, and squid. On Christmas Eve we would celebrate at church, not with gifts, and then we'd go to church again on Christmas morning.

"The types of food served at the holidays varied in Italy. It's different in each of the regions. In Sicily, fish was big, a big part of the diet all the time. Other cities and regions have different things. A lot of the country has *baccala*, though.

"My memories of most of the holiday celebrations are of religion, the saints, going to church, and eating with the whole family sitting around the table. There was a big meal in the middle of the day and a light meal in the evening, and you always ate your salad after the meal. Partying and dancing were big parts of the celebrations—my dad had a phonograph. They were the traditional Italian folk songs, not like today's. But my biggest memories are of the cannolis."

## Professor Philip J. Di Novo

Philip, who lives in Albany, New York, is the founder of the American-Italian Heritage Association. He says: "There is a saying that God gives us memories so we will have roses in the wintertime of life. During the Christmas season, I recall past Christmases and feel a warm glow because they were happy times.

"My father's parents expected us to spend Christmas Eve with them. Christmas Eve in many Italian homes is full of traditions. My grandparents gave me traditions and customs that have enriched my life. When I was young, I didn't realize that I was given roots, a foundation to build upon. My parents and both sets of grandparents have passed away, but memories of them are still very strong. To be honest, none of the Christmases in the last forty years of my life can compare to those spent at my grandparents' house when I was young.

"I recall my grandmother Di Novo making so many *cucidatas* that she had them on sheets on several large beds. *Cucidata* is a traditional Sicilian Christmas pastry. My grandmother made *cucidata* not only for her nine children and their families, but also for relatives and friends.

"*Cucidata* is a must at Christmastime as far as I'm concerned. My wife and I spend Christmas Eve with my two brothers and their families. I'm the only one who makes *cucidata*, and my hope is that my nieces and nephews will carry on this beautiful tradition.

"We set up a beautiful *presepio* as well as a regular Christmas tree. I put up sprigs of greens in the tradition of my ancestors. The Romans were the first to decorate their homes with greens for the pagan festival the Calends of January.

"Oh, the memories I have of past Christmases! It isn't easy to keep our Italian traditions and customs alive. The young don't seem to appreciate them. As an educator, I believe we can educate our young people to value our Italian Christmas traditions and customs. They are therapy for families; they impart security. It is our duty to pass them on to the next generation for continued beautiful and lasting memories. *Buon Natale!*

"Our Italian Christmas traditions are very special to me. My religious faith and my values are in conflict with how Christmas is celebrated today. For me, Jesus is the reason for the season. The birth of the Son of God is the embodiment of all human births. Our Italian Natale traditions are celebrated with praying, feasting, and music. You celebrate New Year with whom you please, but Christmas only with your own. Our Italian traditions center around the family, and that is very important to us.

"Traditionally, Christmas is essentially a religious festivity. The period of preparation is characterized by the Christmas Novena, which consists of a series of church services. They take place every night for a period of nine nights, during which many beautiful Italian Christmas hymns are sung. Based on Italian tradition, Christmas belongs to Gesu Bambino.

"It has been many years since I celebrated Christmas Eve at my grand-parents' home. They have gone to their eternal reward, but what family celebrations we had! In many Italian homes many fine courses are served, as many as twelve to represent Jesus and his twelve disciples. Having the family together on Christmas Eve is a must; it is a night on which we celebrate our family ties. At midnight of Christmas Eve, going to church as a family to celebrate the birth of Christ has been an old tradition with us. We always had great snacks after church. The Urn of Fate is an Italian tradition we still keep on Christmas Eve. It hasn't been easy to get the teenagers in our family to be excited about our traditions, but I feel we have made progress. I hope that in time they too will appreciate our traditions.

"Italian Christmas customs are as varied as the Italian people. They are unique, beautiful, and they belong to us. Christ was born in Bethlehem, in Judea, yet Christmas really began in Italy. Christ's birth was first celebrated in Rome almost three hundred years later, when the Emperor Constantine adopted the new faith of Christianity. Italy has had many years of celebrating Christmas; no wonder its people do such a wonderful job of celebrating Christ's birth."

# 6

# Setting the Christmas Stage

PART OF WHAT MAKES CHRISTMASTIME so magical are the decorations and displays seen throughout the towns, lining the streets, and in the shops and homes. The Christmas lights on the houses and in the trees, lawn displays of Nativity scenes and reindeer-drawn sleighs, and wreaths hanging on doors and lampposts are just a few of the enchanting touches that showcase the essence of the season.

What better way to kick off the Christmas season than to create that special ambience in our lives? In this chapter, we will explore the many ways to bring the spirit of Christmas into our homes through decorating and adding special touches. We will look at traditional and unique Christmas embellishments, specifically those with an Italian background or flair.

The overall effect and the individual components work together to create the Christmas feel in our homes and in our hearts. Putting it all together is an expression of family, nostalgia, religion, style, and sense of fun.

## Italian-Americans Go All Out

Many people believe that the holidays are a big deal, and creating the right scenery is very important to them. Their memories always include the home and its many adornments. Part of the Christmas tradition includes choosing and decorating the Christmas tree, putting lights up on the house, and displaying many different Christmas objects and groupings. There are pine sprigs, pinecones, holly and berries, mistletoe, wreaths, garland, Nativity scenes, little villages, Santas, Mrs. Clauses, elves, reindeer, sleds and sleighs, bells, angels, candles, teddy bears, trains, stockings, candy canes, and carolers—to name a few.

I can think of no better way to get in the Christmas spirit than to pull out those boxes of Christmas decorations and start decking the halls. Not only do the contents illuminate the elements associated with the season, they bring back so many memories.

## My Parents' House at Christmas Time

My parents' house has gone through a couple of different Christmas decorating styles over the years, all of which have become a big part of my Christmas nostalgia. In the old days the house was all decked out with standard red and green, but later it became more burgundy, mauve, and silver with green. Other than that, most of the decorating remained pretty standard.

There was live garland everywhere—wrapped around banisters and rails, around doorways and entrances, and often accented with big red satin bows. There was a small round table with a floor-length red felt tablecloth with cut-out green felt pine trees and real colored lights. There were candy dishes in the shape of Christmas trees filled with candies (foil-wrapped chocolate Santas and snowmen), crystal hurricane lamps with red and green candles inside, and potted red poinsettias.

Other decorations included little Christmas caroler dolls and light-up lampposts; a tiny artificial Christmas tree decorated with white lights and red heart ornaments; the Dalmatian Christmas tree, which hung on the fireplace in the family room and was filled with different Dalmatian ornaments; the tall, skinny artificial tree that I one year wrapped inch by inch with lights (and recently inherited for my home); a little wooden Christmas train with presents as the cargo; crystal bowls filled with potpourri; and a variety of crystal candy dishes filled with pretty Christmas hard candies.

Above a picture frame in the family room hung an arrangement of green leaves; white, deep red, and pale pink Christmas flowers; sparkly berries; and gold metallic ribbon. On the hearth sat a wooden rocking horse with little toys, holly and berries, wrapped presents, and teddy bears glued on the seat, and a ceramic Santa that my mom painted in hobby class—now thirty years ago.

Mom also had a collection of Annalee dolls (Santa, reindeer, elves, and Mrs. Claus). One year, Dad had a great idea to put Santa (along with a stuffed red toy bag with miniature toys hanging out) in a little red sleigh and hang it with fishing wire from the ceiling along with two reindeer leading it (Rudolph in front). It became a tradition ever since.

We always arranged the Nativity scene, which lit up and played music, on the rock hearth. For many years, I would arrange a little village with light-up houses, foam snow, little streetlights, pine trees, and carolers.

Another tradition was adorning oranges with cloves in various designs and then placing them in a gold-edged glass bowl with pinecones, faux fruit, and silver Christmas ornaments.

In the kitchen, Mom arranged pine boughs on the windowsill and on the top of the window, with a gold bow in the middle, and displayed little Hallmark dollhouse ornaments.

We always put up the Advent calendar, which my mom made out of red felt. It had a big green Christmas tree cutout sewn on the top portion and trimmed with sequins. On the bottom half there were little pockets numbered from 1 to 24, and inside each pocket was a different little felt ornament to pin onto the tree each day of Advent.

## Our Tree

When I was young, the whole family would go and pick out the tree. Our Christmas tree usually sat in front of the living room window, covered with multicolored lights and ornaments collected over the years. It was always a trip down memory lane when we opened the boxes of Christmas ornaments, many of which we hadn't seen since the year before, but some we might not have noticed for several years. The collection grew over the years, but we always had our favorites: There were antique glass figures (Santa, a Dalmatian, a snowman, and bulbs); hand-crafted and painted gems that my mom, my brother, and I made (little policemen, firemen, and Santas constructed from clothespins and felt); as well as cut-out wooden rocking horses that we had painted, and the paper-and-Styrofoam ones my brother and I made in preschool. We also treasured the Hallmark collectibles we acquired each year and the glass Snoopy ornaments.

## At My Grandparents' House

Many Christmas Eves were spent at my maternal grandparents' home. The Christmas tree, set up in the formal living room, was all pink and white, with white lights, clear (crystal/glass/plastic) string garland, pink satin ribbon and pink silk flowers, and roses and poinsettias all over. All around the tree were perfectly color-coordinated packages, artistically wrapped. Other decorations included garland over the arched fireplace, with pinecones, white ornaments, and greenery. Above that hung a black wrought-iron wall sconce with three dark green tapers and two little Christmas trees (complete with miniature red and gold balls). On the mantel hung three stockings.

## My Place

When I got married and moved into a home of my own, we acquired many Christmas decorations and ornaments from my family and my husband's family in addition to buying and making many of our own. We have a small, cozy house that is easy to fill quickly with Christmas decor. The tall artificial tree I acquired from my parents fits perfectly in a spot in our living room.

I recently purchased two more skinny trees of varied heights, and arranged a grouping of trees along one wall of the living room. The main, tallest tree is lit with clear and multicolored lights and adorned with our extensive collection of ornaments, from antique glass to wood to plastic. We have decorative balls, Santas, policemen, dogs, brides and grooms, cheerleaders, Snoopy, bells, birds, soldiers, angels, houses, rocking horses, teddy bears, stars, blocks, candy canes, books, fireplaces, snowflakes, reindeer, and musical instruments.

In the left corner, a medium-height tree (with colored lights and a bow on top) sits behind a small wood table filled with presents. On the other side of the wall is my favorite new addition: an Italian Christmas tree. The shortest of the group, this tree is set atop an antique chest of drawers and wrapped with hundreds of clear lights. It's decked out in Italian ornaments, for which I searched all over. I ordered most of them off the Internet. They include a glass Italian Santa, an Italian snowman, a ball that says *"Buon Natale,"* and more.

From the Incredible Christmas Store in New York I found some beautiful hand-painted Christmas balls, one with a scene from Venice and the other of Rome. The ornaments were mouth-blown in Europe, designed by home decor artist Peggy Walz, and hand-painted by skilled artisans following Walz's designs. I made a banner that reads *"Buon Natale"* out of cut-out wood, acrylic paint, and rhinestone accents. I also have a wooden Befana ornament that my parents have had since I was a child. The tree is topped with a Leaning Tower of Pisa, which I made out of a cardboard wrapping paper roll and a tiny round box lid.

At the foot of the tree, I set up an Italian display: an Old Befana doll, an Italian snowman figurine, a Leaning Tower of Pisa block, a Leaning Tower figurine that I received as a gift, and a Venetian gondola, which I bought at a holiday-specialty store. In the gondola, I arranged a little Santa, a gondolier, and lots of goodies.

Other Italian decorations in my home include my own take on a tiny Italian Christmas village, complete with a church-front Nativity scene, as well as Mediterranean and Tuscan touches using fruit displays and grape and vineyard motifs. For the kitchen, which displays vineyard accents

## More Ideas for an Italian Christmas Tree

Use lots of green, white, and red, which are the colors of the Italian flag and of Christmas. Place small Italian flags (paper or cloth) on top or throughout the tree. String individual strands of green, red, and clear lights. For garland and for tying bows to place on the tree, use green, white, and red striped ribbon, or braid together individual thin ribbons in those colors. Make Italian ornaments out of hollowed-out eggshells painted in the Italian flag motif or with little Italian scenes, landmarks, and icons on them.

Another alternative is to adorn your tree in the following motifs: angels; fruit; grapes and vines; wine barrels, bottles, glasses, decanters, corks, and corkscrews; or food items such as pasta, garlic, bread, and sweets.

year-round, I made a small grape-and-ivy tree to place on the table. In one of two bay windows, I have decorated with poinsettias in rustic baskets, a large glass bowl filled with fruit, an assortment of Italian containers, and bottles filled with oil and vinegar. In the other is an arrangement of clear glass vases and canisters filled with different kinds of Christmas candies and dried pasta, as well as a bowl of fruit and a small artificial fruit-studded tree. On top of the refrigerator is another small tree covered with mini candy canes.

The rest of our Christmas decorations consist of a small Nativity scene, many candles and ornate holders, and other touches I will mention later.

# Christmas Decorating Considerations

The first consideration for decorating your home for Christmas is "when." My family usually started right after Thanksgiving. The outside house lights were one of the first additions, followed by all the interior decorations, except for the Christmas tree, which was purchased the first or second weekend in December.

It's a good idea to start the home-decorating process early enough to give yourself time to enjoy it and not be rushed. After all, you're likely to be busy later with all those other Christmas activities, such as shopping, baking, wrapping, visiting, and entertaining. I find holiday decorating one of the most fun activities of the season, allowing for abundant creative expression.

Spreading the process out over several days or weekends is also a good idea. This way you can arrange things just the way you want them, adding elements or rearranging as you go. You might also want to set aside some time to make your own Christmas decorations, as well as look around for new ideas in stores, books, magazines, and friends' homes.

A great way to begin the decorating process is by "priming your canvas," or getting your house ready. Consider a deep cleaning before decorating, and, if possible, declutter as much as you can. Perhaps you can pack away non-Christmas things in the Christmas decoration boxes during the season.

Once your house is clean and the Christmas items have been pulled out, it's time to start decking the halls. You will need to find great spots for your Christmas treasures. You might have a certain arrangement for all your items, or you might want to try something new. Plus, any new items you have acquired will need to be placed as well.

# Italian-American Christmas Decorating Staples

Many of the items we discussed in chapter 4, on Christmas in Italy, can be seen in the homes of Italian-Americans as well. Most common are a

Christmas tree, stockings hung by the fireplace, Christmas and Advent wreaths, Advent calendars, Nativity scenes, candles, garland, Christmas lights, holly, and mistletoe. In addition, many Italian-American homes have *ceppos*, Italian-style angels, symbols of La Befana, and other very Italian items.

# The Christmas Tree

For many, the Christmas tree is the most important Christmas decoration and serves as the holiday focal point. Start by scouting out the best location in your house to showcase your tree. Some possibilities are in front of a window, so that the tree can be seen from the street, against an empty wall, in a corner, in front of a staircase, in the middle of a room, on a table or stand, or temporarily replacing a fixture. Many families place the Christmas tree in a room such as the family room or living room, where opening gifts and other activities will take place. It is often a place where it can be most enjoyed, where people tend to go to relax and congregate. Others choose to display it in a foyer or entryway where people can see it when they enter the house. Still others opt to have more than one Christmas tree in the house.

The space in which you choose to display the tree will determine its size. Measure the area ahead of time so you don't have to guess.

The next consideration is the type of tree to acquire. Artificial or real? Cut or potted and replantable? Douglas or noble fir? Natural or flocked? When you have a good idea of what you want, you're ready to buy a tree, bring it home, and set it up.

## Adorning the Tree

To bring life and magic to a tree, lights are a must. I personally think the more the better when it comes to lights. One year I got into the habit of wrapping lights around every, or almost every, branch. This is very time-consuming and requires many more strands of lights than you think you're going to need. But the end result is dramatic and bright. If you have an artificial tree you only have to do it once, and then you can store it with the lights already on for the next year. I start wrapping from the top and work my way down and around the tree. Of course, you don't have to wrap the lights to make a tree look stunning. You can just place them throughout the tree.

You might want to add garland, ribbon, beads, or some other stringed enhancement to your tree. Wrap or cascade beautiful ribbon around it or tuck long strands of garland here and there.

Next are the ornaments. When it comes to Christmas tree ornaments, the varieties are endless and personalized in every shape, material, color, character, and symbol. There are glass bulbs, Santas, reindeer, snowmen, animals, people, sleighs, little trees, presents, candy canes, cars, trains, books, teddy bears, musical instruments, fruit, and so on. There are Italian ornaments like blown glass, angels, Nativity pieces, religious symbols, and wooden toys, as well as ornaments with an Italian feel—like grapes; vines; assorted fruit; Romanesque objects; red, white, and green striped ribbon and bows (resembling the Italian flag); and numerous icons like La Befana, Babbo Natale (the Italian Santa Claus), little gondolas, and replicas of landmarks like the Leaning Tower of Pisa and the Coliseum.

As a finishing touch, some people like to sprinkle the tree with glitter or confetti or scatter tinsel, twine, angel hair snow, birds' nests, real flowers and plants, paper chains, or strung popcorn and cranberries. Other touches include strung pasta (elbow macaroni, penne, and other tube shapes—either plain, painted different colors, or sprayed metallic sliver or gold, or strands of beads or jingle bells.

At the bottom of the tree, you may choose to place a tree skirt. There are ready-made varieties in many beautiful designs. Or you can make your own using sheets, tablecloths, or pieces of material in your preferred colors. White, metallic silver, or gold give a rich look. You may also wrap large empty boxes of varying shapes and place them around the bottom of the tree.

Top the Christmas tree with something significant—a star, something that lights up, an angel, a doll, a flower arrangement, a large bow, a present, or a pinecone cluster (natural or spraypainted silver or gold).

Suspend objects from the ceiling near the tree. An Italian tradition is to hang angels with invisible string. You can also hang clouds, stars, Santa in his sleigh pulled by reindeer, or La Befana riding on her broom.

## The Nativity Scene

Every Italian home and most Italian-American homes have at least one Nativity scene out at Christmastime. Such a scene usually consists of a manger made from wood and ceramic figurines of Mary, Joseph, Baby Jesus in a crib, Shepherds, three Wise Men, angels, and animals. Some are even more elaborate with hay, paper mountains, paths leading to the stable, lights, and other features.

## The Ceppo

A *ceppo* is found in the homes of many Italian-Americans. This pyramid-shaped frame, often made of wood, sometimes replaces the Christmas tree in Italy. However, many Italians, especially those living in the United States, have both. The *ceppo* can be a couple of feet to several feet tall and consist of different layers, usually three or four. On the bottom and widest level, the Nativity scene is set up. The upper levels are decorated with colored papers, gilt pinecones, little pennants, small gifts, candy, fruits, and other items. The *ceppo* is usually adorned with candles and topped with a star or a doll or other ornament.

## Little Villages

Little villages or street scenes are another popular Christmas decoration. Many Italian families collect them as extensions of their Nativity scenes. These little towns often feature houses, shops, and churches (that sometimes light up), street lamps, waterfalls, ponds, and people.

## An Alternative Ceppo

*Materials*

> Set of three shadow boxes (small, medium, and large) or frames
> Small Nativity set (you can find one at craft stores)
> Fruit (real or artificial)
> Tiny wrapped gift boxes
> Candles and holders
> Decorations of choice

Stack the boxes (or frames), largest to smallest, preferably on a table or shelf against a wall. You can also hang them on the wall. Place the Nativity scene on the bottom tier. Decorate the top two tiers as you wish using the other items. Place candles all around.

Bring more of Italy into your Christmas by creating an Italian village. Use the little buildings you have and arrange them to resemble a little Italian town. Line the houses up, and add a little cobblestone road in front of them. In front of a little church, place a Nativity scene like those seen in front of churches in Italy. You can get really creative and make your own little buildings. Use little wooden or cardboard birdhouses, or transform old village houses with paint and props. Add shutters, balconies, and clotheslines to the houses. Incorporate little shops—bakeries with mini baked goods, produce stands with mini fruit—as well as tiny replicas of Italian monuments and landmarks, such as historic sites, bell towers, museums, cafés, piazzas, villas, and palaces. You can even make your little village look like a particular city or region of Italy: Tuscany, with rolling hills, cypress trees, vineyards, and lots of greenery; Naples, with a little volcano; or Venice, with canals, bridges, and mini gondolas. Or combine many features and represent Italy as a whole.

# Mini Italian Village Scene

## *Materials*

Scissors
Small cardboard birdhouse ornaments (available at various
    arts and crafts stores)
Razor blade (or cutter)
Acrylic paints and brushes
Hard plastic (such as from a container of Q-Tips)
Smearproof black magic marker
Glue
Masking tape
Strand of clear lights
Sheet of white snow/foam
Tiny Nativity scene
Village accessories as you choose (such as mini pine trees,
    Christmas lights, etc.)

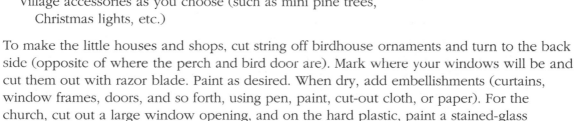

To make the little houses and shops, cut string off birdhouse ornaments and turn to the back side (opposite of where the perch and bird door are). Mark where your windows will be and cut them out with razor blade. Paint as desired. When dry, add embellishments (curtains, window frames, doors, and so forth, using pen, paint, cut-out cloth, or paper). For the church, cut out a large window opening, and on the hard plastic, paint a stained-glass window design. When dry, outline this design with a smearproof black marker and glue on.

    To set up the village, find a large enough flat surface, such as a tabletop or shelf. Set up houses, shops, and church, mark the surface with tape, and remove the buildings. Arrange the strand of lights on the surface, making sure that there is a light near each tape mark. Tape down lights as needed. Lay snow/foam sheet on surface, using additional pieces to create hills in back rows (so that all houses will be seen). Poke lights to be used in little houses through the foam and place buildings in their places. Poke the lights into the bird door holes in the back to illuminate the cut-out windows. Arrange trees and other accessories as you wish. For added touches, use twigs, branches, and rocks from your yard. Create cobblestone roads using tiny rocks (such as the kind for fish tanks).

# Christmas Greenery

In many Italian-American homes, greenery plays a big part at Christmastime and can be seen everywhere. Mistletoe is hung above doorways or on front doors, as ancient Romans once believed that it could ward off evil spirits and bring peace. Garland is hung on stairway banisters, shelves, doorways, windowsills, and fireplace mantels. Pine, ivy, and holly are found throughout the house.

# Christmas Wreaths

One way to display all sorts of greenery, and many other items, is on Christmas wreaths. Wreaths come in all shapes and sizes and can be made of just about anything. From pine—real or artificial—to twigs and vines to plastic foam covered in berries, flowers, or leaves, you can purchase or make the wreaths of your choice and hang them on the front door, inside or out, on walls or mantels, in front of mirrors, on cabinets, in windows, and just about anywhere.

Lights on a wreath add a nice touch. Just take into consideration the cord—where it will plug into the wall and how to camouflage it. Or you can use battery-operated lights so there is no cord to worry about. For lush green wreaths, you may choose to leave the decorations sparse, adding a bow at the top or bottom and maybe a few bulbs or pinecones. Or you might fill them with ornaments, miniature toys, fruit, teddy bears, or whatever you choose.

When making a wreath using plastic foam, you can use a wide variety of materials. Completely cover the foam with leaves, cranberries, flowers (carnations, poinsettias, pansies), hard candy, popcorn, dry pasta, crayons, mini ornament bulbs, mosaic tiles, pebbles, shells, birdseed, or ribbon (wrapped all around). Be creative.

Italian meatballs

Typical Italian holiday table setting

The Christmas after my grandfather died, each of us
received a gold cross in his memory.

Cousin Cindy making
Valentine's Day cookies

Coloring Easter eggs

Italian pasta "houses"

An Italian-style gift basket

Platter of traditional Italian
Christmas cookies

Italian cookies and cakes

Decorating for Christmas—
with food

Happy New Year, Mom and Dad!

Frittata

An antipasto platter, containing
meats, cheeses, and olives

Hand-painted wooden "Buon Natale" sign

A Leaning Tower of Pisa Christmas tree topper

Handmade Christmas tags

A homemade miniature Italian village at Christmastime

Vignette featuring several Italian-inspired Christmas decorations, including La Befana, the kindly, gift-bearing Christmas witch, a miniature *David*, a Leaning Tower of Pisa, and a new twist on Santa's sleigh

Tuscan-style Christmas décor, featuring lots of fruit

Concept for a Christmas tree grouping

A Yule log cake

A *ceppo* made from shadow boxes, featuring the nativity on the bottom tier

Mouth-blown glass ornament featuring Venice scene

Murano glass ornament

Italian snowman and
Santa ornaments

My husband Bobby and me
on Christmas

Cousin Dylan works the
Advent calendar

## Advent Wreaths

Another kind of wreath to opt for is an Advent wreath. For most Italian Americans, Christmas is a time to remember the birth of Jesus, and many do this by celebrating Advent. You can make your own, like the Advent wreaths in a Catholic church, very simply, using a pine wreath, four candles (three violet and one pink), and four candleholders.

Or use wreath-shaped plastic foam, flat on one or both sides. Placing a flat side down, hollow out four holes—one to fit the base of each candleholder. Spraypaint the foam either gold or green and decorate it with pine sprigs or other greenery and decorations as you choose.

Make a miniature Advent wreath using birthday candles. Cut out a small cardboard wreath (using a coffee mug as a pattern) and secure the tiny candles into place with some clay. Glue greenery from the yard, cutout felt pieces, or whatever you choose onto the wreath.

## Decorating with Fruit

Italians have always associated oranges and tangerines with Christmas, using them to enhance their homes at this time of year. Add these citrus fruits, as well as lemons and limes, for a simple yet elegant decoration as well as a nice fragrance. It was always a tradition in my family to decorate oranges with whole cloves, making different designs. Then we would place these oranges in a large bowl along with Christmas bulbs and faux fruit. Try using the cloves to adorn oranges, tangerines, limes, and lemons.

Fruit in general has a Christmassy and Italian look. Arrange assorted fruits (real or artificial) in baskets, bowls, gift boxes, or trays. Mix apples, pears, oranges, lemons, limes, pineapples, bananas, grapes, coconuts, and any other fruit you choose. You can also add vegetables—artichokes, asparagus, tomatoes, corn, and carrots—to your fruit arrangements or create separate vegetable decorations. These are especially great for decorating the kitchen.

## How to Make a Vineyard Tabletop Tree

Use a foam tree mold (such as one in light green that also has a base) and cover it with (artificial) garlands of small-leafed ivy by securing to the top and wrapping around and down to the bottom again and again. After the tree foam is almost completely covered with the ivy, evenly secure miniature artificial bunches of grapes (green, purple, and red). Next, use large wired ribbon—such as sheer purple with a sparkly metallic-gold vineyardlike design—cut into three long pieces and taper, lightly twisting them down the tree on different sides. Tie a large bow, leaving one side very long to taper down the remaining side of the tree. Place the base of the tree in a pot or bowl, and surround with larger bunches of artificial grapes.

Using miniature fruits and vegetables, I made a little produce Christmas tree for my kitchen. I used a twelve-inch plastic foam Christmas tree shape, covered it with metallic green wrapping paper (stapled to the back side), and super-glued the tiny fruit all over it. Then I placed the little tree in a large bowl filled with assorted fruits and vegetables.

I filled a set of three crystal bowls in my living room with rich-looking artificial fruit I found at Michael's. These pieces are actual-size pears, apples, and grapes (in lime green, deep purple, and an orangy red) covered with sparkly velvet. I interspersed the fruit with scented natural and gilded pinecones.

## Tuscan Vineyard Christmas Decor

A great way to decorate for Christmas is to use a vineyard-inspired approach, reminiscent of Tuscany. Incorporate lots of vines, grapes, and ivy into your Christmas decor. You can find all kinds of vineyard designs—garland, wreaths, ornaments, table decorations, and so on.

I found a great ready-made garland of slightly glittery bunches of grapes and bronzy ivy leaves, which I intertwined into an artificial potted tree I have in my living room that is lit with clear lights.

# Christmas Decor Suggestions

- Showcase religious symbols, like pictures and statues of Jesus, Mary, and the saints.
- Feature lots of candles: tapers, votives, tea lights, candelabras, unique holders, floating candles.
- Fill bowls with miniature wrapped presents.
- Place bows above mirrors and pictures; adorn mirror edges and picture frames with garland.
- Decorate chandeliers with grape bunches and sparkly leaves.
- Collect items from nature/your yard, such as twigs and stones, and use them (naturally or spraypainted gold or red, white, and green) in arrangements and displays.
- Hang stars from the ceiling.
- Wrap empty boxes to look like Christmas presents.
- Arrange a grouping of Christmas trees in one area—three, five, or seven trees in varying heights with coordinating decorations.
- String garlands (with big bows in the center) across windows.
- Paint terra-cotta pots Italian-style—green, white, and red—and fill with Christmas ornaments or clove-studded oranges.
- Make Christmas valances for kitchen and bathroom windows using green, red, and white napkins, napkin rings, and curtain rods. You can also paint or stencil miscellaneous designs on them. And you can make the napkin rings yourself with paper towel cores and felt or strung beads.
- Hang little ornament balls in front of windows.
- Re-create Italian Christmas components: *piferari* (shepherd bagpipers) from mountain villages, dressed in crisscross leather leggings, short bulky trousers that are buckled just below the knee, vests of sheepskin, velvet jackets, and peaked caps, and playing sheepskin bagpipes; La Befana with a broom and bearing gifts; Santa Lucia in a white gown and a candle crown; St. Nicholas, Babbo Natale, in a red suit, white beard, riding in a sleigh pulled by reindeer; angels with golden wings (made from hand-glued goose feathers), and halos.
- Make a pasta Christmas tree using a small plastic foam tree shape and different shapes of pasta glued on.
- Create clay ornaments with cookie cutters and decorate with acrylic paint, glitter, jewels, and more.
- String beads and drape them around the home.
- Place little toy musical instruments on the tree, a wreath, or garland.

## Venetian Gondola Christmas Decoration

You can find miniature wooden gondolas/rowboats at many craft stores. I found mine at a place called Stats in Pasadena. It has hooks for wall hanging on the back of one side that is flat, but you can also place it on a table or a shelf low enough for the detail inside to be seen. Fill the gondola with just about anything—pine sprigs or other greenery, pinecones, flowers, Christmas ornament balls, fruit, candles, and so on. I decided to use Santa (or Babbo Natale) being rowed by a gondolier carrying Christmas gifts. To make Santa and the gondolier, I purchased a package of little wooden doll heads with the simple faces already painted on (from Michael's, but also found at other craft stores), chenille sticks in beige and black, and sheets of felt. For Santa, I cut out simple red pants and a shirt and sewed them. I glued white felt trim and pom-poms for buttons. For his hat, I cut out a piece of red felt, fit it onto his head, and stapled it in the back. Then I trimmed the bottom with white felt, and topped it with a pom-pom. I used cotton for his beard, cut-out green felt for his mittens, and black chenille for his boots. For the gondolier, I constructed black pants and a red shirt with white ribbon glued on for stripes and tied around his waist for a sash. I purchased a little black hat and tied a little red satin ribbon around it. I constructed his rowing oar out of brown chenille. I filled the gondola with little assorted wrapped boxes, miniature presents, and toys.

# *More Decorating Tips*

When decorating your house for Christmas, you might want to take your home decor into account and work with the color scheme of your home or individual rooms. Also, find unique ways to add enhancements to every room. For example, for the bathroom, you can find Christmassy soaps, sink fixtures, toilet paper, hand and hanging towels, candles, air freshener, waste baskets, and a magazine rack filled with Christmas books.

For the kitchen, you can utilize food for decorating, such as fruit and vegetable displays, candy, cookies, berries, popcorn, pasta, and herbs. Or use cooking utensils—baking pans, bundt cake pans, cookie cutters (strung like garland), or display Christmas plates, coffee cups, bowls, and trays. Fill clear glass kitchen canisters and jars with nuts, pasta, garlic cloves, and rice leaves, all spraypainted gold. Make a wreath of garlic bulbs. Make breads in various Christmas shapes (for display), as well as cookies and a gingerbread house.

Let each child decorate his or her room for Christmas, complete with their own little Christmas trees to decorate and keep in their rooms. There are many different ways you can decorate the formal living and dining rooms, versus the casual family room or kitchen or dining area.

Bring the spirit of Christmas into your home, and make it as festive as the holidays should be!

## Enhancing the Exterior

When setting the stage for Christmas, the outside of your home is another focal point. What better time to set the right holiday mood than before entering the house? If you're into going all out for Christmas, as many Italian-Americans are, then your exterior living environment will welcome you and any visitors into your home. This can be done many ways—with lights, props, and accessories on the house, surrounding trees and grounds, front door, windows, mailbox, garage, and porch.

Stringing lights on the frame of the house is a common way to infuse the home with Christmas. From the roofline to the outer walls, fences, and gates—outdoor lights can be placed on just about anything. White lights in outside trees and bushes add even more luster. My dad used to outline a large Christmas tree with green lights on the front wall of the house and fill it in with multicolored lights. Other simple light designs could be angels, stars, stockings, gift packages, sleighs, Santa's hat, or snowmen.

Other outdoor enhancements can include outdoor Christmas trees (planted or in pots); garland on the roofline, fences, gates, around poles, light posts, windows, doorways, and tree trunks; wreaths hung on the front door, windows, outside of the house, walls, fences, gates, trees, garage doors, and mailboxes; holiday lawn ornaments like (light-up) Santa, reindeer, and snowmen; lightlines (wire outlines with colored tubes of light) in the shape of Santa, penguins, elves, reindeer, snowmen, a sleigh, or spelling out "Merry Christmas," "Season's Greetings," or "Happy Holidays." You can have these custom-made to say something like *Buon Natale!* " You can also find many props to put on the roof, like Santa and his sleigh and reindeer.

Decorate your front door with wrapping paper and a big bow, and your mailbox with ribbon and ornaments. Hang jingle bells in the trees and hang holiday wind chimes for a soothing holiday sound. Line walkways with luminarias, using paper bags (preferably with wax lining) with some sand on the bottom and votive candles inside. Cut out Christmassy images and glue them to one side of the bags for an added effect. Or use cans (soup or coffee), milk cartons, pickle jars, canisters, or hollowed-out vegetables (like white pumpkins, apples, pineapples, or eggplants) as candleholders. Fill sturdy bowls or jars halfway with water and place floating candles in them.

For pools, Jacuzzis, ponds, and any other bodies of water in your yard, place floating candles directly in the water or get plastic floating bowls and put some sand and votives in them and float them on the water. Other outdoor touches include terra-cotta pots painted to look Christmassy, poinsettias in pots, festive birdhouses and feeders, decorating the doghouse, draping lights on the inside roofs of patios and umbrellas, decorating arbors with white lights, garland and poinsettias, hanging wall sconces with candles on outdoor walls, and hanging candle chandeliers from trees or patio ceilings. Statues, fountains, and gazing balls placed in the yard can add a festive feel as well as an Italian touch.

# Indulging All the Senses

In addition to all of the wonders of Christmas there are to see in your Christmas stage, the other senses play a key role as well. Don't forget about the sounds and smells of the season. (We'll get to taste later, when talking about Christmas foods.)

Music is one of the most essential mood-setting elements of the season. For many people, memories can easily be conjured up by hearing a song of Christmases past. Songs everyone knows and can sing along to have been remade by just about every recording artist. There are the religious songs like "Away in a Manger," "Oh, Holy Night," and "Silent Night." Then there are the fun tunes like "Frosty the Snowman" and "Rudolph the Red-nosed Reindeer."

The Christmas carol is said to have originated in Italy—introduced by St. Francis of Assisi—and has been a major part of the holiday season ever since. Some Italian Christmas carols (*canzoni di Natale*) include: "*Gesù Bambino l'È Nato*" ("Baby Jesus Is Born"), "*Tu Scendi dalle Stelle*" ("You Came Down from the Stars"), "*Mille Cherubini in Coro*" ("A Thousand-Cherub Chorus"), and "*La Canzone di Zampagnone*" ("Carol of the Bagpipers").

A wide range of Christmas music can be found for your holiday listening pleasure, from classical to folk to pop. And many Carols are sung by Italian-American artists, have an Italian flair, or come from Italy. Here are a few suggestions: "Italian Mandolins"; "Mob Hits Christmas," which features festive favorites from a variety of artists including Vic Damone, Jerry Vale, Al Martino, Connie Francis, Louis Prima, Rosemary Clooney, and Paul Anka; "Enchanted Christmas," by Anna Maria Mendieta, with a lineup including "*Gesù Bambino*," "Ave Maria," "Away in a Manger," and "Amazing Grace"; "The Bells of Christmas," a compilation of the Christmas Bells from all over Europe including St. Peter's Cathedral in Rome; and "Venetian Christmas," with Gabrieli Consort and Players.

In addition to these and many more Christmas albums, you can bring the sounds of the season into your home with chimes, bells, and wind-up music boxes.

# Christmas Scents

When most of us think of the scents of Christmas, we are likely to think of the aromas coming from the kitchen—the baking, sauces, and garlic. You can also indulge your sense of smell during the Christmas season by placing various items throughout the house. The small cluster of live pine conjures up images of Christmas. If you don't have a live Christmas tree, you can place pine sprigs in garland, wreaths, on tables, mantels, sinks, and so on. Other ways to capture the wonderful scents of Christmas are with incense, scented candles, potpourri, air fresheners, fresh mint and other herbs, cinnamon, citrus fruit in bowls, and oranges adorned with whole cloves.

# Italian Christmas Decoration Shopping Guide

(The following venues offer a variety of Christmas decorations—as well as gifts. In parentheses, I specified a few Italian specialties, many of which I have purchased from them.)

- Bronner's Christmas Wonderland (Italian Santa ornament, Italian snowman ornament, Italian blessing and Italian prayer ornaments, Buon Natale ornament, Italian snowman figurine). 25 Christmas Lane, Frankenmuth, Michigan 48734; www.bronners.com; 989-652-9931; 800-ALL-YEAR.

- The San Francisco Music Box Company Collectibles and Gifts. www.sfmusicbox.com (Fiber optics Father Christmas/St. Nick, plus angels and cherubs).

- F. J. Designs, Inc., the Cat's Meow Village, 2163 Great Trails Drive, Wooster, Ohio 44691-3738. www.catsmeow.com (Leaning Tower of Pisa wood block from the International Village series, includes a bit of history on the back).

- Christmas Tree Hill. www.christmastreehill.com. 1-800-222-6173 (Old Befana Christmas witch doll).
- Essence of Europe. www.essenceofeurope.com (Three-feet-by-five-feet Italian flag; they also carry an Italian flag license plate frame).
- Collectible Madness, 483 Federal Road, Brookfield, Connecticut 06804. E-mail: cmad@ntplx.net.
- The Incredible Christmas Store and Gift Collection, 30 Rockefeller Plaza, Concourse Level, New York, New York 10112. 1-212-459-1200. www.incrediblechristmas.com (Hand-painted glass ornaments of Venice and Rome).

# 7

# *Spreading Yuletide Cheer*

With the Christmas season comes plenty of opportunities to have fun. People come together to share the joy of the holidays through parties and get-togethers. There is reaching out to others through visits, phone calls, and holiday greeting cards. We show our love with gifts.

Along with all of this comes much planning and preparing—making lists, shopping, cooking, wrapping, serving, welcoming, thinking, and doing. Perhaps the busiest time of the year, Christmas presents many tasks. However, completing these tasks can be a joy in itself.

What are some of the many activities of the season? They include:

- Christmas season parties and entertaining.
- Exchanging Christmas gifts.
- Christmas correspondence.
- Christmas fun.

This chapter will provide creative inspirations for carrying out Christmas tasks.

# Entertaining Basics

Once the home is decorated and the mood is set for Christmas, it is ready to be seen and enjoyed by others. One of the biggest joys of the season is opening our homes to family and friends with numerous parties and get-togethers. And for many Italian-Americans, that means entertaining and feeding numerous guests.

In fact, on any given evening or weekend day in December, it is quite common to have unannounced visitors drop in with gifts or pastries. In my family, this was a regular occurrence throughout the year, but much more so at Christmastime. My parents were entertaining small groups most nights of the week and larger ones on weekends. There was always one big party with all the relatives and many close friends. The meal was usually something Italian—pasta with meatballs or Italian sausage, salad, bread, and several types of desserts—and drinks included lots of wine as well as eggnog, coffee, and liqueurs. A mixture of Italian music and Christmas music was playing in the background, and everyone mingled and had a good time. Later in the evening, there was poker for whoever wanted to play.

I learned a lot about entertaining from my parents—that it was a fun and important part of life, and how to pull it off. You had to have enough room, comfortable quarters, and plenty of food and drink. Plus, the more planning done in advance, the better the event and the easier it would be to pull off.

When planning a holiday party or get-together you must first take care of the preliminaries—where, when, and who. You need to know where your party will be held before you can make any other arrangements. Most likely it will be at your home, but it can also be held at someone else's home, a restaurant, a banquet hall or recreation center, a hotel, or any other location. Then you need to choose a date and time and decide on a guest list. Will it be just immediate family, extended family and friends, couples, parents and kids, coworkers—or everyone you know?

Once you have figured out these basics, it's time to start planning the details—or the "what." What kind of party will it be—small, medium, large, intimate, formal, semiformal, casual, sit-down dinner, just appetizers and drinks, or just dessert and coffee, and so on. If dinner will be served, who will make it? Will you prepare the meal, have it catered, or have everyone bring something? How will the food be served? Buffet/self-serve, passed around family-style, or will you or someone else serve each guest? What kinds of activities will be featured? Will it just be mingling, eating, and drinking or will there be some planned events and entertainment? What about music?

Next comes the "how," as in how you will pull off the party. This includes invitations, coordinating who brings what if it is potluck, deciding on wine or a full bar, who will help you prepare and set up, whether there should be a specific theme or atmosphere you'd like to create, and so on.

## Party-Planning To-Do List

- Decide the date, time, location, and approximate number of guests.
- Decide on theme and level of formality of the party.
- Decide on menu logistics—what to serve, where it will come from, and how it will be served.
- Decide on beverages.
- Compile guest list and send out invitations.
- Plan menu in detail, or contact caterer if necessary.
- Arrange for any entertainers.
- Decide on other logistics—parking, seating, and so on.
- Go shopping for food, beverages, and anything else needed.
- Enlist some help.
- Get the house or location ready—cleaning; making room; getting extra chairs, tables, and dishes if needed; stocking bathrooms.
- Prepare food.

# Planning Tips

Decide where in your home (or other location) you want everything to take place. For a sit-down dinner, will you and your guests all fit around the dining room table, or will you need to set up other tables—and where? For cocktails, appetizers, and self-serve, where will guests sit down and eat? Will you have small tables set up throughout the house? Decide in advance where tables, the bar area, and any other components will be.

Think about your menu. Assuming your fare will be Italian, a few items you might want to make sure you have are garlic, extra virgin olive oil, balsamic vinegar, salt, pepper, basil, tomatoes, Parmesan cheese, mozzarella cheese, bread, pasta, sauce, ground beef, bread crumbs, and onions.

As for beverages, make sure you have plenty of ice, sodas, water, wine, coffee (as well as cream, sugar, and sweetener), and maybe champagne, beer, liqueurs, and hard liquor. For mixers, consider eggnog mix, juices (orange, cranberry, grapefruit), club soda and other sodas, as well as limes, olives, and other garnishes, and stirrers, straws, and bar napkins.

You'll also need to make sure you have plenty of plates (dinner, salad, appetizer, and dessert, as well as bowls for soup), silverware, glasses (wine, champagne, mixed drinks, and water), serving plates and trays, coffee cups, napkins, tablecloths, and place mats.

# Fun Things to Do at Christmas Parties

Most parties present many opportunities to eat, drink, and be merry. These are essential elements at a good party, as are great people; a happy, upbeat, and relaxed environment; and inviting, pleasant, and cozy surroundings, often enhanced by music. More fun things to do at parties include mingling, getting to know people you don't know well, and catching up with those you do. Laughing is a must. If a party doesn't have laughter, it isn't a party. There might be telling of jokes and funny stories, exchanging memories, nostalgia, experiences, sharing kind words, and making future plans to get together.

# Ideas for Holiday Parties

In addition to the standard activities at Christmas season parties, there are several types of activity- and theme-based parties to consider. Many Italian-American people I know host or attend baking parties prior to Christmas. Several women will gather at one person's house on a weekend day and prepare cookies, cakes, and pastries. Each person is in charge of bringing one ingredient—say, ten pounds of flour—as well as mixing bowls and containers. They will often prepare several kinds of dough based on family recipes and either bake the items there or take home the dough to bake later.

It is often women relatives who participate in these baking parties as a family tradition. It's a great opportunity for the younger generations to learn (by doing) the family recipes, and it's also a chance for women to spend the day together. There are also baking parties that include friends, who bring a certain number of their favorite recipes or ones they would like to try and then share them with each other. And there are those that include men and women, often young couples.

Cooking parties during the Christmas season can also be a lot of fun, much like the baking parties. The women will meet at someone's home and cook sauce, meatballs, manicotti, ravioli, lasagna, and any other dish that can be frozen. Another take on this is the cooking party for couples—after which everyone enjoys a great meal together. A gourmet cooking party can be led by a guest chef or teacher.

Wine parties are lots of fun for small or large groups. They can feature wine tasting, a wine dinner (a different wine is served with each food course), or wine trading (a gift exchange of favorite wines).

Music and dance parties can feature recorded music or a live band or musician. A dance floor can be cleared for guests to dance. It's a good idea to have a variety of music—fast and slow—so everyone will want to participate. Karaoke to Christmas songs is also a lot of fun.

At tree-trimming parties everyone helps put ornaments on the tree. This is something my parents would do—invite me, my husband, my brother and his girlfriend, and sometimes a few of the close relatives and friends to come over and have eggnog, wine, coffee, or hot chocolate as we listened to Christmas music and trimmed the tree. This was a way to get their big tree decorated and a fun reason to get together. Afterward, we would have a big meal. Another variation of this could be a tree-trimming party at which everyone brings a small tree and a bunch of ornaments in a motif of choice and decorates together. The host might provide a certain item, like lights, garland, or ribbon.

Holiday open houses allow many guests to casually drop in during a certain time frame. Instead of serving a meal, the host has appetizers and drinks set up for guests to help themselves. This is a great way to have many visitors, but not all at once.

There are also pizza parties, movie parties, holiday brunches, gift-wrapping parties, and craft parties. Just about any fun holiday activity can be a reason to get together and celebrate.

## Special Touches

Compile and display photo albums with photos of each guest from previous parties and get-togethers. Take this one step further and make color copies of the photo album pages to distribute to guests as a keepsake. Display interesting photo arrangements on walls and tables, as well as arrangements of objects. Play games and give out prizes, especially silly ones. Have everyone bring a certain item, such as a holiday photo, Christmas book, or tree ornament to display in a certain location. Have everyone bring a gift, and have a gift exchange. Hold a raffle, talent show, or show-and-tell. Have guests bring a recipe, homemade cookies, Christmas craft, decoration, or ornament, and give a prize for the best one. Play games like poker, blackjack, bocci, board games for kids (with prizes), or go Christmas caroling.

# Christmas Party Themes

In addition to the many types of holiday parties you can have, there are many themes that can be added to tie many elements together, including menu, drinks, decor, table settings, music, activities, favors, attire, games, prizes, invitations, and special touches. While we will talk about many party theme ideas in the last chapter of this book, there are several that are specific to the Christmas season.

## Winter Wonderland

Decorate in all white with lights, candles, tablecloths, napkins, plates, and more, which creates an elegant and dramatic effect. Hang snowflake cutouts from chandeliers, plants, ceilings, and above windows and doors. Use faux snow on windows and mirrors, and decorate with snowy day items such as sleds, ice skates, hats, scarves, mittens, snow boots, snowmen, snowballs, icicles, polar bears, and snow angels. Serve white food, such as chicken, whitefish, pastas with white sauces, clam chowder, cauliflower, white onion, white cheeses (mozzarella, goat cheese, provolone) with crackers, white bread rolls, sour cream dips and chips. Other white food items that might be used to garnish plates are marshmallows, powdered sugar, and grated coconut. For dessert, stick with vanilla flavors and white chocolate. Drinks can include White Russians, vodka tonics, Snowballs (made of gin, Pernod, and half-and-half), and White Alexanders (made with gin, white crème de cacao, and heavy cream). Theme songs can be "Walking in a Winter Wonderland," "White Christmas," and "Let It Snow."

## Jolly Old St. Nick

This theme can feature Santa hats at guest place settings, a visit from Santa, signs designating different rooms as "Santa Claus Lane," "The North Pole," and "Santa's Toyshop." Jolly Christmas music can be played, including "Santa Claus Is Coming to Town," "Jolly Old St. Nicholas," and "Here

Comes Santa Claus." Decor can include red and white striped poles, replicas of Santa, Mrs. Claus, elves, reindeer, a sleigh, and big bags of toys. The table can be set to look like Santa's red suit—red cotton, felt, velvet, or other material with a fluffy white trim on the bottom and a matching table runner down the middle. A shiny black material topped with a big gold buckle (made of cardboard and gold spray paint) could cross the table runner to look like Santa's belt. The centerpiece can be a burlap bag overflowing with toys, as well as miniature toys hanging from the chandelier.

## Martini Christmas Party

This event can feature Frank Sinatra Christmas tunes, martinis in all sorts of festive flavors and colors (mostly red and green), and fun garnishes—mint leaves, berries, candy canes, tiny red tomatoes, and cocktail onions. The drinks list might include Spicytinis (tomato), Strawbatinis (strawberry), and Mintinis (mint). The atmosphere can be Christmas loungy, with low lights and lots of candles. An appetizer table can feature several cocktail glasses of different sizes filled with finger foods like different types of olives, cheese cubes, bits of sausage and ham, nuts, mints, and candies.

## Christmas in Italy

Re-create Christmas in Italy, as discussed in chapter 4, with images of musicians coming down from the mountains, life-size Nativity scenes, La Befana, the Urn of Fate, Tombola matches, and of course, lots and lots of Italian foods.

## Saturnalia Party

Have a party based on the ancient Italian winter solstice celebration, Saturnalia. Props, decorations, and other details can be drawn from the ancient Roman era, and include Roman gods, Saturn, planets, sun, moon, stars, winter, harvest, Yule logs, bonfires, woods, and evergreen. Decorate the setting with greenery, candles, lamps, wood, and Romanesque touches. Have a masquerade where everyone dresses up in elaborate costumes. Elect a Mock King, the Lord of Misrule, or King of the Bean by bean ballot. The menu might be accompanied by bean soups, like minestrone, or split pea soup as well as raisin bread, rum cake, and anything else featuring beans, raisins, and rum. For drinks, serve anything with rum, such as Cinnamon Toast (spiced rum with hot apple cider), Ginger Snap (spiced rum, ginger brandy, eggnog, and a gingersnap), and Roman Punch (dark rum, port, Cognac, raspberry syrup, and lemon juice). Include practical jokes and comedy in the evening's activities. For example, have everyone exchange gag gifts.

### Family Christmas Tree

This is a great idea for a family reunion party during the holidays. Gather as many family photos as you can, and ask everyone to bring photos as well. Gather twigs and branches and spraypaint them gold and/or silver. Arrange them in vases and adorn them with Christmas tree balls, ribbons, pine sprigs, and other ornaments. On some, hang family photos in small gold or silver frames (you can make your own frames using jar lids, Popsicle sticks, or twigs tied with twine). For an added touch, hang faux grape bunches that are sprayed gold or silver and sprinkled with glitter.

For the meal, have each relative bring a dish that is a family recipe. Have everyone exchange family photos and recipes. If you have old family movies, you might play them.

## Prepare for Holiday Drop-ins

During the Christmas season, there are likely to be many unannounced guests, so be prepared. Be sure to have a place set up to entertain that is cleaned up, warm, and comfortable. Have drinks and food that can easily be served to guests on hand such as cheese, crackers, salami, peppers, olives, and various sweets, and items for a quick meal like pasta, sauce, bread, and salad ingredients.

## Being a Guest

When visiting others, whether invited or not, it's always good to bring something. In the Italian culture it is uncommon to show up at someone's home empty-handed. Most people will bring wine, pastries, cookies, or a side or main dish. During the holiday season, many people will also bring the host a Christmas gift.

## Christmastime Is About People

Our connections with others mark the highlights of the holiday season. In addition to hosting and attending holiday parties, dinners, and get-togethers, it is important to show our love, appreciation, and caring by getting in touch and spending time with loved ones. This can be done with a phone call, stopping by for a visit, going to lunch, or spending the day together.

Gestures of kindness this time of year also include reaching out and giving to our family and friends and people in general through our thoughts, prayers, donations of time and goods, cheer, and goodwill, as well as greeting cards and Christmas gifts.

## A Season of Giving

When it comes to Christmas presents, there are many factors to consider—planning, remembering, shopping, choosing, personalizing, buying, making, wrapping, delivering, and giving. It takes a lot of thought and effort to get the right gifts for all of the people on your gift list.

The most memorable gifts I ever received were the ones that had special meaning. As a child, this meant Barbies, dollhouses, bikes, hamsters, and TVs. As an adult, one memory that stands out was the Christmas after my grandfather Tony Marino passed away (the previous April). That Christmas, my mom, grandma, and aunt bought all of the women in the family gold cross necklaces in Grandpa's honor. From then on, we always wore them on holidays.

## Shopping for Christmas Gifts

The earlier you start shopping, the better. Not only will you not feel rushed but you can avoid much of the Christmas shopping crowd. Another good idea is to have a plan. Before setting out to shop, take some time to make a list of all of the people you want to buy for, including family, friends, relatives, bosses, employees, colleagues, clients, teachers, gardeners, housekeepers, mailmen, and neighbors, and jot down ideas about what you might get whom and where you can find that item.

For many of the people on your list, especially those you know well, brainstorm. Write down everything that comes to mind about their likes, hobbies, tastes, wants, things they might have mentioned wanting or needing. Do they enjoy reading, cooking, going to the movies, sports, gardening? You might base a gift on someone's favorite color, food, singer, author, or store. Once you have an idea of what each person might like, narrow it down to a particular store and price range. For immediate family members, it is helpful to have each person make a wish list for you.

Aside from malls, department stores, toy stores, boutiques, and specialty shops, there are many other great places to find gifts. The Internet is a very useful and convenient shopping tool. You can find virtually anything you're looking for from certain books, home accessories, and sporting goods to very specific requests like a work by a particular artist or a lamp from Italy. Some other shopping sources include mail-order catalogs; TV shopping channels; home, garden, and hardware stores; pet shops; florists; drug and discount stores; antiques shops; supermarkets; secondhand stores; candy shops—you name it. And gift certificates can be purchased for anywhere, from craft stores to restaurants, beauty salons, spas, movie theaters, and amusement parks.

## Gift Baskets

Gift baskets are a fun and personal way to present a gift. You can find many types, sizes, and colors of baskets, which can be filled with endless choices of goodies. A smaller, sparser basket can be inexpensive, while a larger, more elaborate assortment can be pricey. Gift baskets are great to give to entire families, business associates, and various individuals on your list. You can purchase them already made up from various gift stores, Italian markets, and gift basket specialists. Or you can have fun, get creative, and make them up yourself, individually choosing each item. If you decide to give identical gift baskets to several people on your list, you might buy items in bulk and separate them into the baskets.

You can find the actual baskets at arts, crafts, decoration, import, and discount stores. Line the basket with paper grass, linens, or foam, and after it is filled, cover it with shrinkwrap or cellophane, or tulle or gauze tied with a ribbon.

Gift baskets can feature a wide variety of items and often follow a theme. Italian variations typically feature food items—from pastas, canned sauces, and cheeses to baked goods, fruit, and candies. You can go with a specific theme, like ingredients for homemade lasagna or sweet lover's delight, or you can create a diverse assortment with a sample of every taste.

Need some ideas for what to include in an Italian gift basket? How about: pastas in all different shapes, including novelty Christmas tree–shaped pastas in green and red; sauces; spices; cooking utensils; tablecloths and napkins (red and white checked or fruit or vineyard designs); salt and pepper shakers; garlic press, candles, and holders; cookbooks; bottles of wine; coffees; liqueurs; bakery items (breads, cookies, pastries); cheeses (Parmesan, pecorino, provolone, mozzarella); salamis; prosciutto; pepperoni; Christmas ornaments and decorations; family recipes and ingredients to make them; nuts (almonds, pine nuts, and chestnuts); raisins; garlic; onions; tomatoes and other produce; jarred sun-dried tomatoes; crackers; Italian salad dressing; dried porcini mushrooms; olive oil; balsamic vinegar; olives; cookie cutters; pickled/jarred/canned products (peppers, artichoke hearts, sardines, and anchovies); beverages like wine, grappa, vin santo, and varied liqueurs; and Italian candies, cookies, pastries, and chocolate-covered espresso beans. Many of these and more items can be found at Italian markets.

Other suggestions for Italian gift baskets include assorted fruit baskets, assorted cheese baskets, wine baskets (with wine, glasses, corkscrew, and stopper), or grape motif baskets featuring items—dish towels, soaps, coasters, napkins, and such—that have grape designs on them.

Gift baskets don't always have to come in actual baskets. Group all of the elements in containers such as boxes (one big box or several stacked variegated boxes tied with a ribbon), suitcases, flower pots, wastebaskets, magazine racks, small bookcases, burlap sacks, big stockings, briefcases, wheelbarrows, mailboxes, ice chests, treasure chests, gift bags, wagons, carts, mini shopping carts, large bowls, hampers, pillowcases, birdcages, or dollhouses.

## Christmas Stockings

Another fond memory from as long as I can remember to present times has been our Christmas stockings filled with goodies. My mom always took the time to find all kinds of fun items with which to fill my brother's, dad's, and my own stocking every year. And each little item was individually wrapped so that opening the gifts in our stockings was prolonged. When I was older, it became tradition for my dad to ask me two days before Christmas to go out and get stocking stuffers for my mom because he didn't know what to get. I would then wrap those goodies and fill her stocking.

For the past few years, I have also been receiving stocking goodies from my mother-in-law, who lives in Colorado and ships them to my husband and me. This last Christmas I did a stocking for her as well, and she was ecstatic, saying she hasn't received one since her mother was alive and made one for her.

# More Gift Ideas

Prior to Christmas, have a party and take a picture of each family member. For Christmas, put those photos in frame ornaments that you decorated (or put in a picture of your family so they will remember you). You could also send these out as your Christmas cards.

If you really search, you can find hundreds of great gift ideas almost anywhere, many of which have an Italian flair. At Rite Aid, I found these great pasta houses filled with pasta. Decorated in Italianesque patterns—grape or tomato inspired—these sixteen-ounce ceramic towers were inexpensive and look great on kitchen counters. At Cost Plus World Market, I found many gift ideas, some of which can be used to fill stockings and gift baskets. Among the items were a stack/tower of multi-jewel-toned velvet boxes filled with gourmet candies; a Leaning Tower of Pisa bottle of dipping oil; a decorative bottle of balsamic vinegar from Modena, Italy; and a variety of Italian cakes, cookies, and candy.

More Italian gift ideas include a bocci ball set; Italian music CDs; Italian movie videos, such as the Godfather collection; gift certificates to Italian restaurants; books, maps, and calendars on Italy; Italian art, collectibles, and imports; Italian food cookbooks; pizza stones; sauce pots; lasagna pans; Venetian glass objects; and anything with a Roman look.

Miscellaneous gift ideas (for just about anyone) include picture frames, holiday ornaments and decorations, live plants, key chains, throw blankets, tablecloths and linen napkins, vases, dish towels, pot holders, corkscrews, wine bottle holders, wine stoppers, decanters, pitchers, wine racks, coasters, stationery, desk sets, soaps, lotions, candles and holders, place mats, book ends, cookie jars, teapots, cookbooks, baked goods, gift certificates, kitchen utensils, barware, assorted flavored coffees, magazine subscriptions, tickets to concerts or plays, salt and pepper shakers, flashlights, night-lights, sewing kits, first aid kits, tool boxes, tools, and small water fountains.

Stocking stuffers can include refrigerator magnets, cosmetics, candies, mints, gum, travel-size toiletries (mini toothpaste, mouthwash, and shampoo), jewelry, toys, lottery tickets, pens, pencils, markers, address books, date books, hair accessories, calculators, bottle openers, dental floss, nail polish, nail files, Scotch tape, Post-its, glue sticks, staplers, staples, film, horoscopes, decks of cards, dice, postage stamps, bubbles, and tiny notebooks.

# Gift Wrapping

Often the way a gift is wrapped is as important and special as the gift itself. There are many ways to wrap Christmas gifts. We have already discussed baskets and alternatives to baskets as one possibility. And of course, there are endless varieties of wrapping papers, gift bags, and decorative boxes to choose from. There are many ways to be creative when it comes to gift wrapping, including the type of paper you use—different textures, colors, thicknesses, designs and patterns, foils and embossed—and the accents you put on top of the paper—the ribbon and gift toppers. You can decorate plain colored wrapping paper (or art paper, newspaper, wallpaper, or paper bags) as well as gift bags with stamps, stickers, cutouts, stencils, sponge painting, rubbings, or gluing on designs made with ribbon, rope, leaves, pine sprigs, beads, twine, or twigs. You can also wrap gifts with foil, fabric, and lace. The possibilities are endless.

As for toppers, you can use flowers (real or artificial), greenery, leaves, little toys, ornaments, photos, picture frames, little presents (made from foam squares wrapped and tied with ribbon), tulle bags filled with potpourri, artificial fruit, scrolls, feathers, candy, and home-

## Leaning Tower Gift Wrap

This works especially well when wrapping a stack of gifts. Anchor the bottom with a large and strong piece of cardboard and stack gift boxes on top of it. Top the stack off with another, somewhat smaller piece of cardboard and pull the entire structure slightly to one side. Use a large piece of white or light gray art or butcher paper to securely wrap the structure, finishing at the top. In darker shades of gray, draw or paint, or cut or paste cutouts, onto the package to achieve the look of levels and arches. Top the package with a tiny Italian flag.

made Christmas items of all kinds. Wrap gifts according to a theme, such as snow paper with a snowflake ornament as a topper, Christmas flowers paper with a large artificial poinsettia on top, or greenery paper with a cluster of fresh pine.

## Christmas Cards and Other Greetings

Sending holiday greeting cards is a great way of keeping in touch. It's always fun to receive Christmas cards in the mail throughout December, and it's nice to know that people remembered and took the time to correspond.

Of course, there are many types of Christmas cards to purchase at grocery, drug, book, and gift stores, either individually or packaged. But you can also have them made or make your own. Family photos on greeting cards add a personal touch and allow people to see those they might not have seen in a while.

Photos can be used in many ways in greeting cards—from actual photos to color or black-and-white photocopies. Places like Kinkos and other printing/copy specialists are good sources for having cards made with your family's photo on them. You can choose from a variety of borders and personalize your message. If you have more time, want to be really creative, or are looking for a fun project to do with kids, why not make your own card/backdrops for your pictures? Using thick paper or cardboard, just trace and cut out a simple shape (ornament ball, Christmas tree, or square frame). For the front page of the card, cut out an opening (circle, square, or rectangle) slightly smaller than the size of the picture. Then decorate the front as you wish, glue the picture into the frame, and

### How to Make Italian Christmas Gift Tags

Using thick white paper, such as water color paper, draw a picture of a Christmas and/or Italian item, such as Santa, tree, wreath, bell, angel, Befana, *ceppo*, Italian flag, leaning tower, or Santa in a gondola. Paint with acrylic paint, then cut out and enhance with rhinestones or glitter. Punch a hole at the top with a tiny hole punch and add string to attach to a gift.

glue another piece of paper behind it. Punch holes at the top of the front and back page of the card and tie them together with a thin ribbon. Write your message on the inside.

# Fun Christmastime Activities

The Christmas season is filled with opportunities to have fun—chances to get out or stay home and indulge in Yuletide activities. One way to enjoy the holidays is to participate in some Italian Christmas traditions.

## Tombola

Tombola, which is played on Christmas Eve in Italy, is a family game similar to Bingo. It consists of a large *tabellone* card with squares numbered from 1 to 90, and several smaller cards with fifteen squares (three rows of five squares), with any combination of numbers 1 through 90 and one blank square. Each player gets a small card, and one person tends to the large *tabellone* card and a box or bag of wooden or plastic *tombolini* with the numbers 1 through 90 on them. The caller pulls out one number at a time and calls it out and then places the number on the *tabellone*. Meanwhile, the players cover the corresponding numbers on their cards using any small object—chips, pieces of paper or cardboard, beans, or orange peel. Five prizes are given to those with the most numbers on the same row. The more numbers in that row, the better the prizes from small trinkets, fruit and candy, to coveted toys, books, games, radios, and money: *ambo* means two numbers on the same row; *terno*, three; *quaterna*, four; *cinquina*, five; and *tombola* for the jackpot, all numbers on the card.

## The Urn of Fate

A popular Christmas tradition in Italy, the Urn of Fate is a fun game of chance in which each person has a turn to take a wrapped present from a large urn or container. While some of the gift boxes contain good gifts, others are empty, or filled with rocks or a gag gift. To add a different twist to this tradition, you might make it a fun way for kids to count down the days until Christmas. Set up an Urn of Fate filled with wrapped inexpensive gifts, and let each child draw one out every day until Christmas.

## Roasting Chestnuts

Roasting chestnuts is a popular Christmas activity all over the world, and has always been an important part of the celebration in Italy. In fact, most chestnuts found in markets for roasting are imported from Italy. Make an activity out of roasting chestnuts, preferably over an open fire—such as a fire pit or fireplace. The stovetop or oven will also do.

There are many kinds of chestnuts, but the best ones are Marroni, which are large and round, and should be a shiny brown without holes or blemishes. You can find them at Italian markets.

Before roasting, cut into the chestnuts with a sharp knife or puncture them with an ice pick (or else they will explode when cooking). To roast, use a chestnut roaster or a popcorn popper with holes in it. Whenever you roast them, make sure to shake the roaster a lot so the chestnuts don't burn and all sides get cooked. Roast for about fifteen minutes, then peel and eat. You can tell that they are done when the skins are pulled back from the nut and they are still firm, but you can stick a fork through them. The meat of the nuts will be soft and sweet. To serve, sprinkle the chestnuts with red or white wine and seasoning (such as salt, pepper, garlic, and spices); dip them into melted butter, melted cheese, oil and vinegar, salad dressing, honey mustard, sweet and sour sauce, chip dips (like spinach and artichoke, sour cream, and onion or ranch); or, for a sweet taste, dip them in honey or sprinkle with sugar, cinnamon, or nutmeg. You can also make up a chestnut trail/party mix with nuts, pumpkin seeds, raisins, and pretzels

## Christmas Activities for Kids

Christmas for the most part is for children, for whom it is a magical time filled with toys, fantasy, and wonder. Most parents will at some time before Christmas take their kids to visit Santa, perhaps have a picture

taken and tell him their wish list. In addition, kids are often involved in decorating the Christmas tree, hanging the stockings, choosing and wrapping certain presents, helping to bake Christmas cookies, making crafts, stringing popcorn, watching Christmas movies and TV specials, reading and having Christmas stories read to them, singing in school holiday plays, looking up to the sky hoping to see Santa and his sled, and leaving milk and cookies out for Santa on Christmas Eve.

Consider hosting a music party (with instruments) for your kids and their friends to sing Christmas carols.

You can also organize an Italian-style Nativity. This is great for kids at school, a recreation center, or at home with friends and cousins. Include a stage or a makeshift stable/manger with large umbrellas or a tent. Have children play the roles of Mary, Joseph, Jesus, the three Wise Men, shepherds, angels, animals, soldiers, musicians, and townspeople. Dress them in simple cloth costumes. Have musicians parade to the manger site (hang a star from a tree above the site). Also have La Befana show up if you choose.

Another activity you might try is to hold a Christmas story time for kids, featuring all kinds of Christmas books, including those about other countries and cultures. Go to the library and let your kids pick some out. Have discussions about the books afterward. One Italian Christmas book suggestion for children is *The Legend of Old Befana*, by Tomie DePaola (Harcourt Brace & Company).

## Christmas Season Outings

There are many ways to enjoy the arts during the Christmas season—concerts, shows, plays, ballets, and musicals among them. One of the most memorable Christmas shows I have seen was the Nutcracker Suite with my mom and grandma. Check with your local paper's entertainment section to find out about upcoming shows and events. Some additional ones might be parades, fairs, festivals, puppet shows, and organized story times for kids.

Spend an evening strolling, sightseeing, and looking at Christmas lights.

# A Time for Caring

During the holiday season, it is important to also remember to go out of your way to help someone else by donating toys, clothes, money, or food to charitable organizations such as Red Cross, Goodwill, or churches. You can also give your time by volunteering and visiting the elderly, shut-ins, and orphaned children.

# Gift Shopping Guide

Many of these sources also carry great items for Christmas decorating

- Rome Gift Shop, 2245 E. Colorado Blvd., #104, Pasadena, California 91107. 1-888-826-5855. E-mail: info@romegiftshop.com.

- Gift Shop Italy. www.giftshopitaly.com. 1-877-644-8790 (Framed art, stationery, gift wrap, journals, desk accessories, and photo albums in Medici and Florentine patterns and more).

- Cademartori's Imports of Italy. www.importsofitaly.com. 1-866-793-9474. (Nouveau silk ties, gift sets such as the Venetian, which includes a tin of caffé del Doge espresso, Brutti e Buoni cookies, *panforte* made in Tuscany, and a tin of Amarelli licorice candy; or the Fab Florentine Taste of Everything, which includes squash ravioli, Sanfaustino sparkling mineral water, fig balsamic vinegar, *panforte* from Tuscany, a tin of Caffé del Doge ground espresso and coffee, a tin of Amerelli licorice candy, sweet Vincott and Sombreroni striped pasta).

- Lovera's Family Grocery Gift Baskets, P.O. Box 313, Krebs, Oklahoma 74554. 1-800-854-1417.

- Eastern Meat Farms, 721 A Franklin Ave., Franklin Square, New York 10010. 1-516-872-3450. www.salami.com (Gift baskets including Antipasto Classico; Sweet Tooth; the Gourmet Sampler; Basket of Treats, which includes imported cookies, candies, chocolates, baci, jelly beans, tea, instant cappuccino, nuts, and *taralli*; the Mama Mia Basket, which the store claims is "the perfect basket to give your mother" and includes many items imported from Italy, such as olive oil, balsamic vinegar, cookies, pastas, coffee, *torone*, nuts, baci candies, jelly beans, and chocolate. Other baskets with various contents are called A Taste of Italy, Grazie Basket, and the Godfather).

- Museo Italo Americano, Fort Mason Center, Building C, San Francisco, California 94123. 1-415-673-2200. www.museoitaloamericano.org. (The gift shop offers books on travels in Italy, Italian poetry, Italian cuisine, and children's books by Italian-American writers, as well as jewelry and ceramics from Venice, Tuscany, and Sicily.)

- Bella Italia Gourmet Gift Basket Company, Inc., 7232 N. Rosemead Blvd., San Gabriel, California 91775. 1-626-287-5674. www.bellabasket.com (A variety of gift baskets featuring wine and gourmet food items, such as the Petite Sampler, the Gourmet, the Sicilian, Bella Bari, the Bella Italia Connoisseur, and the D'Aquino Classic).

# 8

# Italian-American Christmas Foods and Feasts

ONE THING MOST ITALIAN-AMERICANS agree on is that Christmas memories always feature food. They recall grandmothers' kitchens filled with activity and emitting glorious scents of the delicious meal to come, munching on snacks as they anticipated dinnertime, and then sitting elbow-to-elbow around a table almost too small to accommodate the entire family and the numerous food platters.

Being Italian-American, you can't think about Christmas without getting hungry. The feast is how we celebrate, and the focus of the feast, of course, is food. And the food is always delicious and abundant. I can always picture the passing of the many serving dishes and being pleasantly surprised by what is in each one as I help myself to a spoonful, and then being amazed how soon my plate is completely filled.

In the Italian culture, meals bring people together. The dinner table symbolizes family, togetherness, and well being, and food represents everything from love to comfort to celebration. Sharing food is sharing love and happiness. And Christmastime is the best time to do so. Once the plates are filled, the next moments—whether they be forty minutes or three hours, depending on the family—are spent in bliss as everyone eats, toasts, drinks, and chats.

# The Christmas Eve Meal

For some Italian-Americans the Christmas Eve meal is the most celebratory; for others, it's Christmas Day. For most, it's both. Traditionally, the Italian Christmas Eve meal consists entirely or primarily of fish and seafood, usually accompanied by pasta and vegetable dishes.

The Christmas meal often features food from more than one region of Italy. Some families prepare the foods from their ancestors' regions. We will soon explore the influences of various regions of Italy on the types of foods that are served. But first, we will look at some common dishes featured at Italian-American homes on Christmas Eve.

Probably the most commonly prepared Italian Christmas Eve dish is *baccala*, which transcends regional boundaries and has remained a tradition for many families. Because it is preserved, *baccala* is easily transported and stored, therefore increasing its popularity. The salted cod dish is usually prepared several days before Christmas Eve and is served alone or in salads, pasta (like spaghetti or baked ziti), vermicelli, or stew (such as with potatoes and green olives).

Squid, or calamari, is another favorite Christmas Eve fish. It is often served boiled, baked, roasted, marinated, fried, or stuffed. My family always had stuffed squid, which they called *sache*, with spaghetti and red sauce. It is made from the squid's bodies, which are cleaned thoroughly and then stuffed with a bread crumb mixture. Some people prepare a red calamari sauce, which they serve over fettuccini or in a salad or soup. Calamari can also be featured as part of an antipasto platter, rather than as a main dinner dish.

Some other traditional fish dishes are *capitone* (female eel), which is marinated, fried, or roasted; smelt, usually fried; as well as many variations of octopus, clams, shrimp, cod, sole, flounder, swordfish, lobster, anchovies, sardines, crab, scallops, oysters, mussels, halibut, and tuna. The menu might include scallops over angel hair pasta, baked stuffed shrimp, shrimp scampi, fettuccini with smoked salmon, fried cod, snail salad, spaghetti with red clam sauce or red shrimp, grilled salmon, *spigole al forno* (baked bass), *bavette al tonno* (pasta with tuna), spaghetti *alle alici* (spaghetti with anchovies), *caponata di pesce* (fish salad), or fish soups.

Side dishes include every kind of pasta—from spaghetti to rotelli to lasagna—as well as vermicelli. There is also a wide array of salads and vegetables such as broccoli, eggplant, zucchini, artichokes, asparagus, and more. Vegetables are served many different ways, including steamed, boiled, roasted, grilled, sautéed, fried (especially broccoli, artichokes, zucchini, and eggplant), with sauces, and mixed with pasta. Breads, bean dishes, casseroles, fried mozzarella and ricotta, soups, and wine can also be found in abundance on the table. After dinner, dessert is served with coffee (and sometimes after-dinner drinks) and features platters of fruit— apple slices, kiwis, oranges, pineapple, and so on—and numerous sweet breads, pastries, and cookies.

## The Christmas Day Feast

Many people I know, my family included, celebrate Christmas Day with a turkey feast. Families come together and often repeat the activities of the night before, only with different types of foods and often earlier in the day. My family always ate dinner around three or four in the afternoon on Christmas Day. Grandpa Tony was always in a hurry to eat.

We had the usual side dishes—stuffing, mashed potatoes, cranberry sauce, yams, green bean casserole, and salad. Several families I know add lasagna and other pasta dishes to this meal. Other common Christmas Day dishes include prime rib, pot roast, ham, lamb, Italian sausage, sides of potatoes—roasted, rosemary, scalloped, or potato salad—and baked beans, soups, and various salads.

## Preparing for the Christmas Meals

Unlike the pre-Christmas dinner parties and get-togethers, the Christmas Eve and Christmas Day feasts usually consist of the same traditional fare each year, making them easier to plan. You already know what will be served. However, preparing the meals can be very time-consuming and take a lot of work. There is the shopping, the precooking prep work, the cooking and assembling, the serving, and the cleanup.

In my family, the preparation for Christmas Eve began weeks prior with my mom and grandpa discussing the menu—which usually stayed pretty much the same—specifically the *sache*. They would call around to find the best place to buy the squid, go together to purchase it about three or four days before Christmas, and then spend the day before Christmas Eve cutting, skinning, and cleaning it thoroughly. My grandma would make the stuffing, which the three of them would stuff into the bodies, and then my grandma would sew up the squid and cook them in the sauce. Meanwhile, my parents would shop for the Christmas Day turkey and accompaniments and prepare those as well.

## Christmas Feasts Checklist

*Appetizers:* antipasto platters filled with cheeses, marinated vegetables, salamis, and/or seafood; fried mozzarella and zucchini; stuffed mushrooms; vegetable trays with dips; mini pizzas

*Breads:* garlic bread, rolls, focaccia, bread sticks, tear bread

*Soups:* clear broths, fish soups, bean soups like minestrone, clam chowder, vegetable soups

*Salads:* green salads with Italian dressing or oil and vinegar, pasta salads, potato salads, antipasto salads

*Vegetables:* broccoli, asparagus, artichokes, eggplant, zucchini, squash, potatoes, yams, peppers

*Pasta dishes:* lasagna, manicotti, stuffed shells, spaghetti, linguini, ziti

*Seafood:* mussels, clams, shrimp, scallops, fish

*Meats:* beef, pork, lamb, game, poultry

*Other dishes:* cheeses, polenta, stuffing

*Desserts:* fruits, sweet breads, cookies, and pastries

*Beverages:* wine, coffee, nonalcoholic drinks, liqueurs, cocktails

# Christmas Sweets

Sweets are an important part of the Italian Christmas and can be considered a tradition themselves: *"I dolci."* There are many types of cookies, pastries, and sweet breads that are associated with Italian Christmases—in both Italy and America. In many households you will find a seemingly endless assortment of delectable treats made with ingredients that often include honey, nuts, raisins, cinnamon, and spices. In fact, it is said using nuts in the sweets is supposed to be good luck, as they are thought to bring fertility. Honey is said to ensure sweetness in the year to come.

Some Common Italian Christmas treats include:

*Strufoli:* Honey pastry balls from Naples, often arranged in cone-shaped mounds and decorated with tiny candies

*Cenci:* Pastry ribbons fried and sprinkled with powdered sugar

*Spumetti:* Chocolate hazelnut meringues

*Torrone:* Nougat candy made with toasted hazelnuts, honey, and sugar that come in many varieties from soft and chewy to hard and crisp

*Cannoli:* Pastry shells filled with a sweet ricotta cheese mixture, wrapped again with dough, fried, and sprinkled with powdered sugar and chocolate shavings

*Pandoro:* A veronese golden bread cake, which is naturally leavened and is said to be the food of angels. It is in a star shape and sprinkled with powdered sugar

*Panforte:* A gingerbread made with hazelnuts, honey, and almonds that is a specialty of Siena

*Panettone:* Traditional Milanese bread, naturally leavened and filled with raisins, candied fruit, and sultanas

*Pandolce:* A butter cake with raisins, pine nuts, hazelnuts, and candied orange peel. It is a specialty of Genoa

*Mostaciolli:* Cinnamon bread biscuits with chocolate from Rome

*Pignolata:* Honey clusters

*Casssata:* Sicilian cake

Italian cookies are made in many varieties: fig cookies, spice balls, amaretto cookies, sesame cookies, pine nut cookies, *cucidata* (Sicilian fig cookies), *biscotti* (hard, toastlike cookies flavored with nuts, anise, cinnamon, and other spices, and good for dunking in chocolate, wine, or coffee), and many others.

## Pre-Christmas Baking Rituals

The cookies and pastries are part of the Christmas tradition and are a must at every holiday gathering. In order to bake a wide variety of these sweets, many people will set aside an entire day or more and make a fun event out of it. In many Italian-American families, the women will get together several days prior to Christmas and bake dozens of varieties of cookies.

"About two weeks before Christmas, we get together—me, my sister, my daughter, my nieces, and my mother—and spend the whole day making all the doughs. Everyone takes each kind of dough home to bake," says Sandi Bastianelli. "We always make sesame cookies, Russian tea, *biscotti, pizzalles*, and now a lot of American cookies, too. Now our younger generation wants to learn . . . one niece wants to start in October."

In my family, the baking rituals involved my mom and me (my brother, too, when we were kids). We would spend hours making detailed sugar cookies out of homemade dough with cookie cutters in many shapes—Christmas trees, ornaments, stockings, candy canes, Santa, reindeer, snowmen, gingerbread men, elves, sleighs, bells, presents, houses, stars, soldiers, wreaths, and more. We then applied colored frosting with paintbrushes. I still have many of the cookie cutters that my mom (some even her mom) had as a child. We also always made our favorite chocolatey, butterscotchy, and nutty seven-layer cookies, and my mom would also make various Italian cookies. We also purchased an array of Italian cookies and pastries from an Italian market to feature on the dessert tables.

# Christmas Tables

An important part of the Christmas feast is where everyone will sit and eat together. With most big Italian families, it is almost impossible to host the gathering unless you have enough space to accommodate everyone and places for all to sit. This means a large dining room table and/or enough smaller tables (and room for them) and chairs to put together to make a big table.

My parents' house had a large dining room with a table that seated twelve. Because the dining room opened into the living room, we were able to set up another table close enough so that everyone was still in the same room and able to eat together. After gathering at the main table for grace, we all passed the serving platters from table to table.

The dining table (or tables) had important rituals attached as well, which included how it was set. The main table was set with a forest green silk tablecloth, covered with a white Christmas lace one, napkins that matched the bottom cloth, Spode Christmas tree china, gold silverware, and crystal wineglasses. It was my job (once I was old enough) to set the table.

The centerpieces always varied, and often it was my task to create one using Styrofoam, sprigs of pine, pinecones, little ornaments, and ribbon. It was either a wreath shape with a hurricane lamp in the middle, a little sleigh from which the evergreen sprung, or a cluster of greenery, flowers, pinecones, and ornaments. There were always candles to either side in festive candleholders (such as brass flute/trumpets). The chandelier was also decorated with garland, ribbon, and pine sprigs. The kids' table often resembled the big table, minus the centerpiece and sometimes with Christmas place mats (such as red and green presents adorned with satin ribbon).

You can find great Christmas centerpieces at supermarkets, florists, or gourmet and specialty stores, or you can simply make your own or use decorations you have in your house. Here are some ideas: bowls of glass ornaments and/or pinecones with accents of pine, holly and berries, and ribbon; wreaths; Advent wreaths; Christmassy flowers in vases (such as poinsettias, tulips, roses, carnations, amaryllis, or Christmas cacti); small Christmas trees; Nativity scenes; villages; statues; fountains; and wishing balls.

You can also coordinate table setting based on the various party themes/motifs that we discussed in chapter 7. For added ambience, play some mood-setting dinner music and put out personalized place cards.

## Pairing Italian Wines with Meals

While many wines overlap, here are some suggestions. As a rule, red wines work well with meats, red sauces, and strong cheeses, while white wines work best with fish, white meats, and white sauces. Sweet wines go best with desserts and sweets. It's more of a preference than anything else, and at most holiday feasts there is an abundance of both red and white wines.

The best all-around Italian wine for most meals is Chianti, as it goes with most Italian foods. Chianti is a bright ruby to deep red, dry, full-bodied wine that is soft, subtle, and smooth with an aroma of violets and flavors of cherries and raspberries. This quintessential wine from Tuscany is best when the bottle says *"Riserva,"* meaning it has been aged at least three years. Some varieties include Chianti Classico Villa Primavera, Chianti Sigillo, and Chianti Classico Villa Antinori. A favorite of mine is Ruffino Chianti Classico Riserva Ducale 1995.

A good wine with Christmas Eve fish meals, specifically *baccala*, is Torbato Terre Bianche, which is a fruity, dry, warm-bodied white wine. Another good one with fish is Verdicchio, a greeny-gold white wine.

To go with Christmas Day turkey, try Marzemino, a harmonic and alcoholy white with the flavors of blueberry and strawberry. And with roasted chestnuts, the light red wine Cagnina di Romagna is a good choice. Another good white wine (an Italian-American wine from California) is Coppola Bianco (by Niebaum-Coppola), a blend of chardonnay, muscat, and malvasia.

For a nice white wine to go with pork and ham, try Chardonnay

Grave, which is dry, delicate, persistent, and fruity, with flavors of pineapple and apple.

Wines to go with dessert and fruits are: Vin Santo—white, warm, soft, full-bodied, slightly sweet, and great for dipping cookies into; Aleatico dell'Elba—red, warm, rich, sweet, sharp and subtle, which is good by itself or with cakes and biscuits; and Cagnina di Romagna—red, sweet, served with cookies and sweets.

Following is a breakdown of many Italian wines according to what types of food or particular dishes they accompany well. (You can refer to this list when planning other meals throughout the year as well.)

*White wines that work well with appetizers or light meals:*

- Dry and fruity wines like the lively and delicate apple-flavored Galestro
- Slightly bitter and apple-flavored Terre di Franciacorta Bianco
- Slightly acidic, light-bodied Gavi, with flavors of flowers, fruit, and green apple
- Tannic Agorà, with flavors of white fruit
- Full-bodied pineapple-flavored Vernaccia di San Giminiano
- Full-bodied yet soft Muller Thurgau, with flavors of pear and white peach
- Full-bodied, soft, slightly bitter, pear-flavored Orvieto Classic secco
- Light white wines like the fresh and fruity Vermentino di Alghero

*White wines that pair well with poultry, fish, and seafoods:*

- Dry and flowery wines like full-bodied, delicate, and lightly flowery Vernaccia di San Gimignano
- Fresh and balanced Verdicchio dei Castelli di Jesi
- Trebbiano d'Abruzzo, a dry, full wine with delicate flavors of apple
- Lemony Fiano di Avellino

- Dry, soft, apple-flavored Greco di Tufo
- Falanghina, which is full bodied, with flavors of peach flower and yellow fruit
- Trebbiano di Ravenna, a soft, dry, and fruity wine
- Regaleali, dry, soft, and warm with flavors of fruit and grapes
- Chardonnay, which is dry, fresh, balanced body, fruity with flavors of pineapple and apple
- Locorotondo, a dry, very warm white, with flavors of white fruit
- Pinot Bianco, which is soft with balanced body and flavors of apple and peach
- Brezza, which is fresh and flowery
- Orvieto Classico, a dry, soft, harmonious, fruity wine
- Soave Classico, a white that is dry, slightly alcoholic, flowery

*Red wines that go with cheeses (most of these wines also work well with grilled meats, first plates, and various pasta dishes):*

- Lambrusco di Sorbara, a soft, dry red
- Barbera d'Alba, a red that when aged, has a rose flavor; slightly acidic, not very tannic, and good with sweet Gorgonzola cheese
- Barbaresco, a burgundy with orange reflex; soft, tannic, rose flavor, good with "Fonduta" Italian cheese
- A wine that goes with very aged and mature cheeses is Vino Nobile di Monterpulciano, which is dry, delicate, with a hint of violets
- Cabernet Franc is dry, fruity, tasty, tannic
- Grignolino is dry, tasty, slightly tannic, spicy, with flavor of rose
- Barolo is dry, tasty, tannic, spicy, with flavor of rose
- Casteller is tasty, tannic, with balanced body and fruity
- Wine that goes well with semistrong cheeses is Rupicolo di Rivera, a soft, dry red, which is moderately tannic

*Red wines that go well with roasted red meats:*

- Brunello di Montalcino is intriguing and harmonious, soft, velvety, smooth, with a strong hint of toasted almond. It is aged four years before selling and becomes *riserva* at five years
- Aglianico is dry, soft, full
- Cannonau di Alghero is dry, full, fruity and with balanced body

*For grilled meats:*

- Cabernet Sauvignon Grave, which is dry, tannic, fruity, delicate
- Refosco, a dry, tannic, fruity red
- Barbera del Monferrato La Monella, which is fresh with good body, fragrant, and has a red fruit smell

*For game:*

- Rosso di Montalcino, a dry, slightly tannic red, fruity with flavor of raspberry
- Brunello di Montalcino, a dry, soft, fruity red
- Schiopettino, which is dry, soft, fruity

*For veal:*

- Terre di Franciacorta, which is harmonic, very delicate, smells of flowers

*For lamb:*

- Merlot, which is winey, complete, dense, full, with the flavor of pepper and vegetables

# Liqueurs

Some common Italian after-dinner liqueurs to serve alone or with sweets are:

- Amaretto, which is made from apricot pits and has a rich, almond flavor
- Anisette, which is flavored with anis seed and has a licorice flavor
- Galliano, which is flavored with herbs, roots, and spices
- Strega, which is made from herbs and flowers, and has a golden color, and a sweet, mild, flowery flavor
- Nocino, which has a walnut flavor
- Frangelico, a hazelnut flavored liqueur
- Grappa, a version of brandy made with grape skins and seeds left over from wine fermenting that has a fresh taste with fruity aroma
- Sambuca, which is aniseed-flavored, and sometimes served with coffee beans floating in the glass.

# Foods from All Regions

Let's take a look at some of the cuisines from the different regions of Italy. You may want to include certain dishes in your Christmas feast based on the region of your ancestry. The regions are (from north to south): Piemonte and Valle D'Aosta, Liguria, Lombardy and the Lakes, Trentino-Alto Adige, Venice and the Veneto, Fruili-Venezia Giulia, Emilia-Romagna, Tuscany, Umbria, Marche, Rome and Lazio, Abruzzo and Molise, Campania, Puglia, Calabria and Basilicata, Sicily and Sardinia.

Campania (specifically, the city of Naples) has been dubbed the capital of Italian cooking. It is the home of pizza and marinara sauce. Puglia is known for fava beens, figs, grapes, melons, and almonds. The region of Lombardy and the Lakes (specifically, Milan) is famous for the spice saffron. Dishes that contain the spice are often called *"alla Milanese."* Sicily brings us couscous, orange salads, and abundant seafood. From Emilia-Romagna comes balsamic vinegar. Venice is known for risotto, pine nuts, raisins, pumpkins, spinach, asparagus, red leaf lettuce, peas, pomegranates, and seafood. Liguria gives us chickpeas and spinach. And each region has its specialties and popular ingredients, recipes and varieties for appetizers, soups and stews, breads and pizzas, cheeses, vegetables, pasta dishes, fish and seafood, meats, desserts, wines and liqueurs.

## Regional Appetizers

An appetizer from the region of Piemonte is a rich hot dip made with butter, olive oil, garlic, anchovies, and cream. It is a variation of fondue used to dip vegetables in and called Bagna Cauda. From Campania comes *croccheto*, potato croquettes with mozzarella. Or from Piemonte and Valle D'Aosta, *fonduta* (fondue). Some popular appetizers from Sicily are rice balls, fritters, and tiny pizzas.

## Regional Soups and Stews

A few suggestions are: *fricando* Piemontese stew; *cacciucco*, a Ligurian bouillabaisse; *pasta e fagioli* from Campania; *stracciatella*, a soup with eggs, Parmesan, and parsley from Lazio/Rome; *soupe à la valpellineuntze*, a soup with cabbage, from Piemonte and Valle D'Aosta; *soupe à la cogneintz*, a soup with rice, from Piemonte and Valle D'Aosta; *minestrone alla genovese*, from Liguria; *ciupin*, fish soup also from Liguria; *burrida di seppe*, cuttlefish stew from Jiguria; *minestrone* from Tuscany; *Brodetto*, fish broth, from Marche; *zuppa di pesce*, a fish soup flavored with saffron, from Marche; *zuppa di Pesce*, fish soups, from Puglia; fish stews from Sardinia; *zuppa di datteri*, a soup made with razorshell clams, from Liguria; *la casoêula,* a pork stew, from Lombardy and the Lakes.

## Regional Breads and Pizzas

From the region of Piemonte, or specifically Turin, comes *grissini*, or breadsticks. From Liguria, there is focaccia, which is pizza/bread with herbs inside, sometimes flavored with sage, rosemary, and olives. From Abruzzo and Molise comes *pizza con foglie*, a pizza topped with greens and boiled pork. Of course, from the pizza capital Campania, specifically Naples, comes *pizza napoletana/marinara,* with tomato, garlic, and basil—and no cheese; small pizzas topped with tomtato and mozzarella; and calzone stuffed with ham and cheese or vegetables. And from Sardinia comes *carta da musica,* parchmentlike wafers, as well as chunky loaves of bread.

## Regional Cheeses

When adding cheeses to your menu, consider where they originated or are abundant: Parmesan comes from Emilia-Romagna (Parmigiano-reggiano); pecorino, a cheese made from sheep's milk and often served with pasta, from Abruzzo and Molise; pecorino and ricotta cheese from Puglia; ricotta forte, an unusually strongly flavored cheese that goes well in sauces with pasta, is from Puglia; burrata, a tear-shaped mozzarella shell filled with a heart of shredded mozzarella and cream, comes from Puglia; sheep's milk pecorino is the most widespread Tuscan cheese; ricotta cacioricotta, mozzarella, burrata (delicious, soft, creamy, cow's milk cheese), caprini (small fresh goat's cheese preserved in olive oil), and fagottini (small smoked cheeses) all hail from Puglia; mozzarella, caciocavallo, mature provolone and pecorino, and strong cheeses like matured ricotta are from Calabria and Basilicata; pecorino, provolone, caciocavallo, and sheep's milk ricotta are from Sicily; cheeses made from ewe's milk that are either fresh and herby or pungent and salty, like the famous pecorino sardo, come from Sardinia; grana Padano, like Parmesan, comes from Lombardy and the Lakes, as does mascarpone, a smooth and rich cheese used in sweet dishes, and Gorgonzola.

## Regional Vegetables and Vegetable Dishes

White truffles (the shavings of them) melted in a fondutat with fontina cheese and used in pasta or risotto come from Piemonte and Valle D'Aosta. Cardi, raw artichokelike thistle, also comes from Piemonte. From

Abruzzo and Molise, we get diavolini, little hot red peppers (little devils). From Lazio/Rome come fried artichokes (*carciofialla giudia*). Artichokes (*carciofi*) are the most famous Roman vegetable, and are served *alla romana* (stuffed with garlic and Roman mint and stewed) and *alla giudea* (flattened and deep fried in olive oil). From Piemonte and Valle D'Aosta come porcini mushrooms and chestnuts. Spinach is a popular vegetable from Tuscany (and is often mixed with ricotta to make gnocchi). In Umbria, shavings from truffles are used in many dishes. Tomatoes, fennel, and mushrooms are abundant in Marche. Puglia is famous for olives, almonds, tomatoes (often green and sun-dried), and cauliflower. From Calabria and Basilicata come eggplant, tomatoes, olives, and peppers. Wild fungi come from Lombardy and the Lakes.

## Regional Pastas and Pasta Dishes and Sauces

Popular pasta dishes from various regions range from simple ones with light sauces to those stuffed with meats and cheeses and mixed with seafood. Piemonte presents ravioli stuffed with meat or cheese. From Liguria comes Genoa's pesto sauce served over linguine. A fresh tortellini stuffed with ricotta cheese, beef or veal, bread, chicken, nutmeg, and fresh herbs comes from Emilia-Romagna. Pastas served with shrimp scampi and lobster, or chickpeas and hot peppers, or porcini mushrooms, as well as ravioli Rodrigo (stuffed with fish) comes from Calabria and Basilicata. Green pasta and polenta, *pizzocheri* (buckwheat noodles), and various stuffed pastas come from Lombardy and the Lakes.

From Emilia-Romagna comes lasagna, tortellini stuffed with ricotta cheese and spinach, pumpkin, or pork, and other fresh pastas served with *ragú* (meat sauce), cream sauces, or simply butter and Parmesan (*alla parmigiana*). Tuscany presents pasta with beans—white cannellini or borlotti beans (*uoni e lampo*). Spaghetti from Rome and Lazio comes with dressings like *aglio e olio* (oil and garlic), *cacio e pepe* (pecorino and ground black pepper), *alla carbonara* (with beaten eggs, cubes of pan-fried *guanciale*—cured pork jowl—or bacon, and pecorino or Parmesan), and *con le vongole* (clams). Also from this region comes *alla ciociaro* (with *guanciale*, slices of sausage, prosciutto, and tomato) and *bucatini all'Amatriciana* (thick spaghetti with tomato and *guanciale*). Campania's pasta is served with a tomato sauce made with fresh tomatoes, basil, and garlic.

Puglia's pasta includes *panzarotti alla barese* (pockets of pasta stuffed with *ragú*, egg and cheese, or ricotta and prosciutto, that are deep-fried in olive oil). Spaghetti *con le sarde* comes from Sicily. *Culigiones* (large ravioli filled with cheese and egg) and *maloreddus* (saffron-flavored, gnocchi-like pasta) come from Sardinia.

## Regional Fish/Seafood

*Cappon magro* is a pickled fish with vegetables from Liguria. From Abruzzo and Molise comes squid stuffed with anchovies, bread crumbs, and garlic. Rome and Lazio have *baccala*. In Campania, you'll find *polpette di baccala* (small balls of mined salt-cod, fried or served in a fresh tomato sauce). Fish from Calabria and Basilicata is grilled and served with porcini mushrooms. Also from there come *frutti di mare antipasti*— seafood antipasto—and swordfish *involtini*.

Liguria features fish in *carpione*—marinated in vinegar and herbs. From Umbria come trout, crayfish, eels, pike, tench, and gray mullet. Clams with garlic and oil (spaghetti *alle vongole*) is popular in Campania, as are mussels with hot pepper sauce—*suppa di cozze*—and fresh squid and octopus. Swordfish is big in Calabria and Basilicata. In Sicily there is an abundance of anchovies, sardines, tuna, and swordfish served with pasta. And the island of Sardinia is known for its seafood, especially lobster grilled over open fires scented with myrtle and juniper, and *bottarga*, a version of caviar made with mullet eggs.

# Regional Meats

The following meats are common in the following regions: *bollitimisti*—mixed boiled meats—from Piemonte; *culatello*—sausage—from Emilia-Romagna; lamb dishes (especially grilled or roasted) from Abruzzo and Molise; *bistecca alla Florentina*—thick grilled steaks seasoned with salt and pepper—from Florence/Tuscany; *saltimbocca*—veal scallops cooked with ham, and veal *involtini*—from Rome/Lazio; pork, rabbit, and lamb from Puglia; a cold stuffed veal from Liguria; osso bucco—shin of veal—and *bollito misto*—boiled meats—from Lombardy and the Lakes; *bollito misto*—boiled meats such as flank of beef, trotters, tongue, spicy sausage—from Emilia-Romagna; salami (*lucanicche*)—thin slices of salt beef, game, and rabbit—from Trentino-Alto Adige; pork from Venice and the Veneto; ham, pork pot roasted in milk, muset sausage boiled and served with lentils or polenta from Friuli-Venezia Giulia; parma ham—*prosciutto di Parma*—from Emilia-Romagna; grilled meat and char-grilled steak, *arista*—pork loin stuffed with rosemary and garlic—and *pollo alla diavola*—chicken flattened, marinated, and then grilled with herbs—from Tuscany; pork—hams, sausage, salami, and *la porchetta* (whole suckling pig stuffed with rosemary or sage, roasted on a spit), game pigeon, pheasant, thrush, and guinea fowl from Umbria; rabbit, lamb, *porchetta*—whole roast suckling pig—from Marche; *abbacchio*—roasted lamb with rosemary, sage, and garlic—*scottadito*—grilled lamb chops—and *saltimbocca alla romana*—thin slices of veal cooked with a slice of prosciutto and sage on top, served plain or with a Marsala sauce—wild boar, hare, pigeon, rabbit, and pheasant from Rome/Lazio; lamb from Abruzzo, Molise, and Puglia; pork from Calabria and Basilicata; suckling pig from Sardinia.

# Regional Sweets and Desserts

*Bocca di Leone* pastry and *torta di nocciole* (hazelnut torte) come from Piemonte. *Torta di riso* (a sweet, thick rice pudding) comes from Emilia-

Romagna. *Sfogliatelle* (flaky pastries stuffed with ricotta and candied peel) come from Campania. Liguria (specifically, Genoa) brings us *pandolce* (sweet bread with dried fruit and nuts), as well as several *tortas* and pastries. Lombardy and the Lakes bring us two Christmas favorites—biscotti flavored with nuts, vanilla, and lemon; and *panettone. Soffiato trentina* (a meringue trifle) and *zelten trentino* (a rich fruitcake flavored with grappa and usually eaten at Christmas) come from Trentino-Alto Adige. Tiramisu, *baicoli*, and *mandolato* come from Venice and the Veneto. *Cantuccini* (hard almond-flavored biscuits dipped in a glass of Vin Santo), almonds, macaroons, and *panforte di Siena* (a Christmas favorite) come from Tuscany. Umbria has many chocolates and pastries. Marche has *cicercchiata*—balls of pasta fried and covered in honey and frappé. Campania brings *sfogliatella* (a flaky pastry case stuffed with ricotta and candied peel). Sicily is famous for its sweets, such as *cassata* and cannoli (fried pastries stuffed with sweet ricotta and rolled in chocolate). Sardinia has an abundance of light and airy pastries, often flavored with lemon, almonds, or orange flower water.

As we've discussed, food is an important part of Italian-American life and plays a major role in holiday celebrations. The foods featured at Christmastime are a tradition in themselves. And while traditional recipes vary from family to family, one thing is for certain: most families have at least one recipe (usually more) that has become synonymous with the season. For many, these recipes were passed down from ancestors and may have changed somewhat in the process. After all, many Italian cooks teach via hands-on participation, allowing the student to see and feel the process. Plus, many directions call for a "pinch" of this and a "dash" of that, resulting in slight variations of the recipe each time it is made. Nevertheless, the dishes are always wonderful. Here is a collection of some traditional Christmas recipes from several Italian-Americans.

*9*

# Christmas Recipes

## Ingredients to Have on Hand

*Items that Last a Long Time*
- dried pasta
- extra virgin olive oil
- balsamic vinegar
- wine (for cooking)
- at least two big cans of tomato sauce
- whole, crushed, or chopped tomatoes
- at least two cans of tomato paste
- dried sweet basil and other dried spices (parsley, rosemary, thyme, and marjoram)

- Parmesan cheese
- salt and pepper
- garlic salt
- garlic powder
- bread crumbs
- canned olives
- artichoke hearts
- marinated mushrooms

*Fresh ingredients*
- garlic
- onions
- Parmesan, ricotta, mozzarella, provolone, and romano cheeses

| fresh herbs and spices | *Baking Ingredients* | *Cooking Ware* |
|---|---|---|
| bread loaves | flour (white and wheat) | small, medium, and large sauce pans |
| meats | sugar (white granu- lated, brown, and powdered) | skillet |
| vegetables (including tomatoes, mush- rooms, artichokes, peppers, eggplant, asparagus, and broccoli) | eggs | strainer |
|  | baking powder | ladle |
|  | baking soda | wooden spoon |
|  | yeast | sharp knives |
| fruit (oranges, grapes, pears, figs, and anything in season) | canned milk | mixing bowls of many sizes |
|  | graham cracker crumbs | cookie sheets |
|  | nuts | baking pans and dishes |
|  | chocolate | casserole dishes |
|  | dried fruit | rolling pin |
|  | cinnamon | flat surface stone |
|  | liqueurs | electric mixer |

# Appetizers

## Mini Christmas Pizzas

12 pieces white sandwich bread
¼ cup butter, melted
½ cup spaghetti sauce
1 cup shredded mozzarella cheese

¼ to ½ cup of each: onions, red and green peppers, chopped (optional)

Cut white bread with cookie cutters (stars, rounds, Christmas trees, triangles). Brush with melted butter and toast in toaster oven or broiler until lightly toasted/golden. Remove and top with pizza or spaghetti sauce, sprinkle with shredded mozzarella cheese, followed by chopped red and green peppers and onions if preferred. Bake at 350 degrees about 5 to 10 minutes, or until cheese is bubbling.

# Christmas Eve Fish Dishes

## Stuffed Squid

1 loaf French bread
2 pounds squid (you can order these
    from your grocer)
2 large cans tomato sauce
1 can tomato paste
1 large can whole peeled
    tomatoes

2 to 3 eggs
¼ cup chopped fresh parsley
Salt and pepper to taste
3 cloves garlic, minced

Break up bread into chunks and dry overnight. Clean squid in cold water and place in a bowl. Pour the cans of sauce and paste into a stockpot and heat. In a large bowl, mix all other ingredients with your hands. Stuff squid with mixture. Do not overstuff, as the squid really plump when cooked. Secure with toothpick (or sew with needle and thread, and remove thread after cooking). Drop stuffed squid into boiling sauce and simmer for 20 to 30 minutes. Remove squid from sauce, handling with care, as they burst easily. Drain sauce and serve immediately.

### How to Clean Squid

Remove the head and tentacles. Empty the sac and rinse completely. Place squid in hot water and peel off the outer veiling. Rinse squid again in cold water.

## Fried Calamari

1 pound squid, cleaned well
1 to 2 cups flour, seasoned with salt
    and pepper

2 cloves garlic, minced
4 tablespoons olive oil

Cut squid into rings or small pieces. Coat pieces with flour. Fry in hot oil with garlic on all sides until golden brown. Drain on paper towels. Serve immediately with marinara sauce.

# Crab Manicotti

2 6-ounce cans fancy white crab-meat, drained
3 eggs, beaten
1½ cups Italian seasoned bread crumbs
2 tablespoons Parmesan cheese
1 cup mozzarella cheese, grated
½ cup cottage cheese
½ teaspoon garlic salt

½ teaspoon black pepper
1 teaspoon basil
1 8-ounce package manicotti, prepared according to directions on package and cut into halves vertically (you can also use jumbo shells)
1 cup tomato/spaghetti sauce

Mix crabmeat, eggs, bread crumbs, Parmesan, mozzarella (reserving some to sprinkle over manicotti before you put it in the oven), cottage cheese, garlic salt, pepper, and basil in a large bowl. Stuff pasta halves with the filling and place in a baking dish (with a thin layer of sauce on the bottom), drizzle stuffed manicotti with remaining sauce, and sprinkle with mozzarella. Bake at 350 degrees for about 35 minutes, or until cheese is bubbling.

# Lori's Seven Seafood Pasta Dish

2 tablespoons olive oil
2 tablespoons butter
2 tablespoons garlic, minced or chopped
⅓ pound fish steak, such as halibut, cod, swordfish, or tuna (cut in bite-size chunks)
¼ cup shrimp
¼ cup preshucked oysters

¼ cup scallops
⅓ pound whitefish, such as red snapper, sole, flounder, or sea bass (cut in bite-size chunks)
¼ cup littleneck clams
¼ cup squid (cut into rings)
4 cups linguine, cooked
1 cup tomato-based pasta sauce

In a large skillet, heat olive oil, butter, and garlic. Add fish steaks and shrimp, and cook 2 minutes. Then add oysters and scallops, and cook 2 minutes. Next add whitefish and clams, and cook 2 minutes. Then add squid and cook 3 more minutes. Serve fish mixture over linguine and top with tomato-based sauce.

# Sautéed Scallops Over Angel Hair Pasta

2 tablespoons olive oil
2 to 3 cloves garlic, minced
1½ pounds jumbo scallops
1 teaspoon garlic salt

½ teaspoon black pepper
¼ cup white wine
1 package of angel hair pasta,
    cooked

Heat oil in skillet. Add garlic, scallops, garlic salt, and pepper. Cook about 5 minutes. Add wine and simmer uncovered about 5 minutes (until scallops are cooked through, opaque in the middle). Toss with pasta.

# Shrimp Scampi

⅓ cup olive oil
3 cloves garlic, minced
1 teaspoon salt
½ teaspoon pepper
½ teaspoon basil
½ teaspoon oregano

2 pounds jumbo shrimp (shells
    removed)
1 pound pasta, cooked and drained
1 teaspoon parsley
Parmesan cheese, grated

Heat oil in skillet. Add garlic, salt, pepper, basil, oregano, and mix. When garlic is lightly browned, add shrimp, and cook until shrimp are golden brown (about 5 minutes). Serve over pasta and sprinkle with parsley (and Parmesan cheese if desired).

# Gina Schaffer's Pasta With Shrimp and a Wine Cream Sauce

1 tablespoon butter
1 small onion, chopped
1 clove garlic, minced
1 cup white wine

1 cup heavy cream
1 pound shrimp
Salt and pepper
1 pound pasta, cooked and drained

Heat butter in a sauté pan and add onion. When browned, add the garlic, white wine, and heavy cream. Heat to thicken. When sauce has slightly thickened, add shrimp and continue to boil sauce for 2 to 3 minutes. Add salt and pepper to taste. Mix pasta with sauce.

# Grilled Shrimp Skewers

Bamboo skewers
2 pounds jumbo shrimp
2 tablespoons olive oil

1 teaspoon garlic salt
1 teaspoon pepper
1 teaspoon Lawry's seasoning salt

Skewer shrimp, about 3 or 4 on each stick. Brush both sides of shrimp with olive oil. Mix garlic salt, pepper, and seasoning salt together, and sprinkle on both sides of shrimp. Cook on grill about 3 minutes per side, or in broiler about 5 minutes per side.

# Claro's Fried Cardune

1 stock of *cardune*
2 fresh lemons
Eggs
Flour

Seasoned bread crumbs
Vegetable oil for frying
Salt and pepper

Clean *cardune* as you would celery, peeling any extra strings. Add a little lemon juice to a large bowl of water and put *cardune* in this bowl as you clean them. The lemon keeps them from turning black (you should dip your hands often also or they will turn slightly blackish). Cut the cleaned *cardune* into 4-to-6-inch pieces and place into a large pot of water with the juice of 1 lemon in it, and turn on high heat. When the water comes to a boil, continue cooking until *cardune* pieces are tender, but not mushy, about 30 minutes to 90 minutes. Drain and rinse with cold water. Pat dry with paper towels and prepare your coatings. Make one bowl with sifted flour, then another with beaten egg, then one with bread crumbs. Dip the *cardune* in the flour, egg, and bread crumbs, shaking off extra bread crumbs. Continue till all pieces are coated. In frypan, heat oil till hot and place *cardune* pieces in one at a time and fry till golden, then turn over and brown on both sides; place on paper towels to drain. Salt and pepper to taste and serve.

# Barbara Lando Stead's Spaghetti Pie

| | |
|---|---|
| 1 pound spaghetti | 2 tablespoons melted butter |
| 1 cup milk | 1 cup Parmesan cheese, grated |
| 9 eggs | Pepper to taste |

Preheat oven to 325 degrees. Cook spaghetti and drain. Mix remaining ingredients in large bowl. Toss spaghetti with half of egg mixture. Level spaghetti in greased square pan (a glass dish works best, but metal can be used). Pour remainder of mixture over spaghetti evenly. Bake for 30 minutes, or until it is firm and puffs high. Pie will fall as it cools. Cut in squares; serve warm or cooled.

"Christmas holds many traditions in the Stead house, but Christmas Eve is a favorite of ours. As the whole family is busy getting ready for Santa's arrival, holiday parties, and Midnight Mass, my mom somehow finds time to whip up a batch of spaghetti pie. She has been making this Italian favorite every year as long as we can remember, and probably long before that. As soon as it is out of the oven, everyone in our family is burning our mouths on this savory treat. This indulgence has always meant more than simple enjoyment; it represents spending time with family at our favorite time of year."

MICHELLE AND AIMEE STEAD

# Christmas Sweets

## Grace Bastianelli's Italian Biscotti

1¾ cups sugar
1 cup margarine or butter, very soft
4 eggs
Rind of 1 orange
1 teaspoon orange extract

2 tablespoons anise extract
3 cups flour (more if needed for firm dough)
3 level teaspoons baking powder
1 cup toasted almonds or walnuts

Cream sugar and margarine and add eggs. Add orange rind, orange extract, and anise extract. Add sifted flour with baking powder and mix until smooth. Add nuts. Put mixture on floured board, adding more flour a little at a time to make a firm dough. Preheat oven to 375 degrees. Line cookie sheet with foil and make three long strips from dough (be sure to space dough about 4 inches apart). Bake for 15 to 20 minutes. Slice diagonally 1 inch apart and put back on cookie sheet with open side up. Put under broiler a few minutes.

## Sandi Bastianelli's Sesame Cookies

½ cup margarine
½ cup butter
4 cups flour
1½ cups sugar
1 teaspoon baking soda
1 teaspoon salt

1 egg
½ cup oil
1 tablespoon vanilla
¼ cup water
⅓ cup sesame seeds
Jam

Melt margarine and butter; put flour, sugar, baking soda, and salt in a large bowl and pour melted margarine and butter over dry ingredients. Mix together to form fine particles. In a small bowl, beat egg, oil, vanilla, and water. Add to flour mixture and mix well. Stir in sesame seeds and mix well. Form dough into small balls (about 65 to 70) and place on ungreased cookie sheet. Make indentation in center of each ball and fill with jam. Bake at 375 degrees for 10 to 12 minutes.

# Strufoli (Honey Clusters)

2 cups sifted flour
¼ teaspoon salt
3 eggs
2 teaspoons vanilla extract

1 cup olive oil
1 cup honey
2 tablespoons sugar
Powdered sugar

Mix flour, salt, eggs, and vanilla extract in large bowl. Knead dough until smooth. Roll out into long thin rolls, and cut off about 1 inch at a time. Roll into tiny balls. Heat oil in skillet or stir-fry pan (or use deep fryer if you have one), add dough balls, and fry until golden brown all over (constantly rolling them in the pan to cook evenly). Remove and drain on paper towels. In a separate pan, heat honey and sugar until very hot, about 5 to 10 minutes. Remove from heat. Drop in dough balls and stir until all balls are entirely covered in honey mixture. Remove balls from pan and chill in the refrigerator about 10 minutes. Take them out and arrange them into clusters. Sprinkle with powdered sugar. Refrigerate.

# Granieri Date Bars

¼ cup margarine
1 cup sugar
2 eggs
1 teaspoon vanilla

1 cup flour
¾ teaspoon salt
1 cup dates, chopped
1 cup walnuts, chopped

Cream sugar and margarine. Add well-beaten eggs and vanilla. Sift flour and salt and add. Fold in dates and nuts. Bake in an 8-inch square pan at 350 degrees for 45 minutes.

# Claro's Lemon Drop Cookies

½ pound margarine, softened
1 cup granulated sugar
6 eggs
½ tablespoon lemon extract

5 cups flour
1 tablespoon baking powder
Powdered sugar
Lemon juice

Preheat oven to 375 degrees. Cream margarine and sugar together. Add eggs and lemon extract and beat well. Add flour and baking powder. Mix until dough holds together well. Roll into approximately 1-inch balls. (Be careful: Too thin cookies will not look right; too thick and they won't coat well.) Bake 10 to 15 minutes or until slightly brown. Allow to cool. Make frosting by mixing powdered sugar with lemon juice until you achieve a thickness that you like. Dip cookies into frosting.

# Claro's Almond Biscotti Cookies

1 pound margarine
1½ cups granulated sugar
6 eggs
½ teaspoon anise oil

5 cups flour
2 tablespoons baking powder
1 tablespoon salt
1 cup almonds, coarsely chopped

Preheat oven to 350 degrees. Cream margarine and sugar together. Add eggs and anise oil and beat well. Add flour, baking powder, and salt. Add almonds. Mix all ingredients well. Divide dough into three pieces and roll into logs about 2 to 3 inches in diameter. Place on greased cookie sheet and bake for about 20 minutes, or until lightly golden. The baking time will vary, depending on the diameter of the rolls. Allow to cool, then slice each log into ½-inch-thick slices. Place cut side up on cookie sheet and bake again until golden brown.

# Claro's Chocolate Spice Balls

6 ounces soft margarine
1¼ cups granulated sugar
2 eggs
1 tablespoon vanilla
½ cup strong coffee
3 cups flour
2 teaspoons baking powder
¼ cup cocoa
1 teaspoon ground cinnamon
1 teaspoon ground cloves
¾ cup ground walnuts

## Frosting

2 cups Hershey's unsweetened
   cocoa
½ cup powdered sugar
½ cup strong coffee

Preheat oven to 350 degrees. Cream margarine and sugar well. Add eggs, vanilla, and coffee slowly, and beat well. Add dry ingredients and spices, and beat well. Roll into small balls and place on lightly greased cookie sheet. Bake for about 10 to 12 minutes. Allow to cool.

Mix sugar into cocoa. Add coffee to sugar and cocoa mixture a little at a time until the frosting has the proper consistency. Dip cookies into frosting and allow to cool.

# Mom's Famous Seven-Layer Cookies

½ cup melted margarine in a 9-x-12
   pan
1½ cups fine graham cracker
   crumbs
1 (6-ounce) package chocolate
   chips
1 (6-ounce) package butterscotch
   chips
1 small can Angel Flake coconut
½ cup nuts
1 large can condensed milk

Layer ingredients in pan in order indicated above. Dribble milk on top. DO NOT MIX. Bake at 350 degrees for 30 minutes, or until done. Cool in pan. Cut into small squares.

# Mom's Snow Balls

1 cup butter or margarine
½ cup powdered sugar
1 teaspoon vanilla
1 cup chopped nuts (pecans are
    best)

2½ cups flour
Powdered sugar

Cream butter and sugar together. Add vanilla and nuts. Add flour, and mix. Form into balls ¾ inch in diameter. Bake at 350 degrees for 12 to 15 minutes. While still warm, roll in powdered sugar.

# Mom's Easy Pie Crust

1 cup flour
1 tablespoon sugar

½ cup melted butter

Put flour and sugar in pie pan. Add melted butter. Mix with fork right in pie pan. When completely mixed, pat down and shape with hands.

# 10

# Italian-American New Year's Celebrations

FOR MOST ITALIAN-AMERICANS, New Year's is another holiday spent with family over a huge feast. The contents of the feast vary from family to family, but almost always feature many courses. Many of these dinners include Italian foods for one, some, or all the courses. Activities often include many of the usual holiday practices—eating, drinking, chatting, laughing, celebrating, listening to music, and sometimes singing, dancing, and playing games.

However, the focus of the celebration now turns to welcoming the approaching year and all the hope and possibility it brings. There is an Italian proverb: *"Anno nuovo vita nuova."* It means "The New Year calls for a new way of life." Friends and relatives come together to ring in the new year together. The negative aspects of the old year—grudges, ill will, bad habits—are left behind to make room for the wonderful things to come.

Resolutions are often made—either privately or out loud at the party. Sometimes each person at the table will take a turn to share his or her resolution or a hope, wish, prayer, or blessing for the new year. The old year isn't forgotten entirely—only the negative parts of it. It is common to toast and remember the good and significant events that took place over the year and to express gratitude in order to build on them in the year to come.

At midnight, everyone raises a glass of champagne, cheers, toasts, kisses, and hugs. The party becomes even more festive—the music gets louder and livelier, and noisemakers are sounded. Streamers and confetti fly through the air along with bubbles and balloons. The celebration often lasts well into the dawn.

## New Year's Eve Memories

Like all other major holidays, my New Year's Eves growing up (and many in my adult life) were spent with family, and took place at my parents' home—the gathering place. My parents always loved having company and entertaining, and their home was always warm, cozy, and welcoming. Their food was always delicious and plentiful, and their parties were always fun. On New Year's Eves when I was a child and throughout high school, we used to get together with another family (who had kids about our ages). Some years the guest list also included several other friends and relatives.

Meals were large, and varied from year to year. They often featured steak and seafood along with many side dishes. We always made a round cake, which we frosted and decorated to look like a clock with the hands at midnight. The adults drank champagne and the kids drank Martinelli's sparkling cider. Music was played all night long, and the TV was tuned to the Times Square New Year's Eve special.

When it got close to midnight, we'd turn the music off, the TV up, and begin to count down, all with our silly hats on, drinks in one hand and noisemakers in the other. At midnight we jumped around, made noise, and then grabbed some pots and pans and went out into the street banging them together and yelling "Happy New Year!" (My parents often ended up with dented pots and pans and would have to buy new ones.)

When we came back we played "Auld Lang Syne," and sang along. It was always a great time, and one I came to appreciate. When I was a senior in high school I thought I was too old to spend New Year's Eve with my family, so my friend Tami and I went to a dance club instead. By eleven o'clock we were bored, left, and made it back to my house in time to catch the final countdown, fill a glass with champagne, and ring in the new year family-style.

Many other Italian-Americans I talked to have similar memories of New Year's Eves spent at home with family and friends, having a big feast, and engaging in some traditional practices. Several also remember the incorporation of Italian customs and foods.

Josie Vinci's New Year's Eve celebrations took place at home and included a big meal and playing cards. "If you didn't have the right card, someone would say '*Moshkoni*' and put ashes on your cheek," she remembers.

Dorothy Pantleon says, "My mother always made pizza, and we used to stay home and not go anywhere. We just sat around and ate." Her family also would eat *caponatena* (eggplant) with bread.

Restaurant owner Rina Mele spends New Year's Eve cooking at the restaurant, where there is always a big New Year's Eve dinner. Afterward, she and her family have dinner, which includes lentils, and ring in the new year. On New Year's Day, the family has another big dinner.

David Manzari, who grew up in Bari, Italy, and moved to the United States seven years ago, reminisces about the festive New Year's Eve celebrations in Italy. "New Year's Eve is also St. Sylvester's Night," he says. "We would have a big dinner of *zampone* [pork leg, smoked] surrounded by lentil beans, which represent richness. In Italy, at midnight, big fireworks displays took place everywhere. You couldn't even go outside because you might get hurt—it was a big thing. We also had *torrone* [crunchy hard bars with almonds], cookies, and pastries that were all homemade."

Along with the festivities that Italian-Americans share with many other cultures, many traditions from Italy are still practiced by many. We will look at some of the New Year's traditions in Italy, many of which are embraced by Italian-Americans and can be incorporated into your celebrations.

# New Year's in Italy

In Italy, New Year's is an extension and an important part of the Christmas celebration. The Yuletide activities continue through New Year's Eve and New Year's Day, and go on to Epiphany.

One thing that sets the Italian New Year's Eve apart is that it falls on the feast night of St. Sylvester. It is believed that on New Year's Eve St. Sylvester, who was pope when Constantine declared Christianity the official state religion, therefore putting an end to paganism, closes the door on one year and its pagan ceremonies and opens the door to a new year in a Christian era. Putting behind the old year and embracing the new is reason for great rejoicing in Italy. The New Year's celebration represents hope that the new year will bring many good things.

On New Year's Eve, more big feasts take place with a wide variety of foods. Some symbolic Italian New Year's foods are lentils, raisins, and oranges, all of which are symbols of riches, good luck, and the promise of love, health, and fortune. Honey, another popular New Year's food, represents a sweet new year to come.

Panettone (the sweet bread often eaten at Christmas) and other sweet breads and cakes, like *torciglione*, are eaten as symbols of hope and prosperity. While the New Year's Eve menu varies according to region and individual preference, many feasts include pork and beans. Some common dishes include *cotechino* (fresh pork sausage) with stewed lentils, *zampone*, Italian sausages, pork chops, stuffed capons, sauage *brovada* with sweet-and-sour turnips, stuffed leg of veal, veal osso buco, turkey, fish, beef steaks, lasagna and other pasta dishes, gnocchi, cheese, *lessata* (soup with grains, beans, and garbanzos), breads (such as the round bread *cannizzu*, with a ladder, which is a symbol of good luck), and desserts like *mustazzola*, *pignolate*, *cucidata*, biscotti in many forms (such as covered with sesame seeds or plain for dipping in chocolate sauce), *strucolo* (strudel), and *torta di mele*.

At midnight, people toast with Italian sparkling wine (like Asti Spumante), as fireworks are set off throughout the towns. Many people also throw the old things they no longer need out the window, which represents eliminating the negative aspects of the old year. All kinds of noises can be heard everywhere—people cheering, screaming, yelling, clapping and stomping, fireworks exploding, gunshots and cannons firing, church bells ringing, glasses and pottery breaking, objects hitting the ground, and champagne corks popping. The noises are believed to chase away evil spirits before they have a chance to intrude upon the new year.

## Ideas for Celebrating New Year's Eve

New Year's Eve is a great opportunity to bring together family and friends for a festive time that can be casual, elegant, formal, traditional, creative, simple, involved, or whatever you choose. You can celebrate with a sit-down dinner with family and serve traditional Italian New Year's food, such as pork and lentils, or throw a large party for numerous people with cocktails and finger foods. There are many ways to incorporate Italian traditions into New Year's celebrations—with foods, themes, and activities.

One way to incorporate an Italian tradition is to have an outdoor party around a bonfire (bonfires, torches, and candles are often included in New Year's celebrations in Italy). At an outdoor party, you could serve some great hot cocktails, like mulled wine punches, and coffee drinks and barbecue some skewered appetizers. As it might be very cold outside, you might want to start this party

### Other Italian New Year Traditions

- Holding a bunch of coins in one hand while the clock strikes twelve to ensure an increased fortune in the new year.
- Giving loved ones jars filled with honey, dates, figs and bay branches, or figs wrapped in laurel leaves, to wish them sweetness and good fortune in the new year.
- Sending flowers to loved ones.
- Parents giving their children money and gifts.
- Hanging mistletoe on doorways for good luck and health.
- Lighting candles as a symbols of brightness in the new year.
- Having bonfires, burning the Yule log, and lighting torches.

early—around five or six in the evening—and as it gets later, move the party inside. However, there are ways to work around the weather. You could rent or buy tents in various sizes, with side flaps that can be rolled down or secured up, and heat lamps.

For the bonfire: You might already have fire pit built into your yard, but if not, you can buy (or rent) portable ones that come in many different styles, sizes, and price ranges. Several vendors specialize in them. One such vendor is Fire Sciences Inc., in Williamsville, New York. Fire Sciences has everything from indoor/outdoor fireplaces to bonfires and fire pit kettles as well as torches, lanterns, and heat lamps. Scattering torches and lanterns throughout the yard also adds a nice touch.

You could also hold your bonfire indoors around a fireplace as your focal point. Set up plenty of seating as well as appetizers near the fireplace to encourage guests to congregate there. And don't forget the Yule log. The Italian tradition is to keep it burning until New Year's Day.

For added indoor ambience, consider dimming the lights and using plenty of candles throughout the house.

## *Decorating*

Many people leave up the Christmas decorations for New Year's—and maybe add a couple of New Year's elements such as paper plates, napkins, and cups in a New Year's design, a tablecloth and centerpiece on the table, some streamers and balloons around the house, and so on. We used to decorate the dining room chandelier with balloons and streamers and scatter confetti all over the table.

Some other ideas for decorating for a New Year's Eve party include using traditional Italian symbols for this time of year—holly, evergreen, and mistletoe, which might still be up from Christmas anyway.

Or you can incorporate a "Twelve Days of Christmas" motif with pears everywhere. (You could also include faux birds on branches and twigs, birdcages and birdhouses decorated creatively.) In addition to pears, add other fruits and vegetables for a Tuscan feel. Arrange pears, artichokes, and pineapples on tables and shelves or in bowls, baskets, and trays along with oranges, lemons, limes, apples, grapes, and other types of fruit. You could also mix pinecones, ribbon, and glass ornaments in with the fruit.

Go with a festive, colorful look with bright flashes of red, royal blue, turquoise, yellow, orange, purple, emerald green, and hot pink scattered around. Use draped scarves, ribbons, balloons, streamers, pillows, tassels, and other touches. Place festive pinecones spraypainted in different colors and glittered in bowls with sequins, streamers, and glass balls. Make props and centerpieces out of Styrofoam, papier mâché, or cardboard, and cover them with flower petals.

Decorate in all silver, all gold, both silver and gold, or black and white. Coordinate tablecloths, napkins, plates, centerpieces, props, and other elements accordingly. Or use stars as your motif—hanging from ceilings, chandeliers, stairways, windows, doors—or suns and moons (or all three for a celestial motif).

Set up a festive dance floor complete with disco ball, fluorescent lights, strobe lights, spinning and flashing lights, and black lights. Other dance floor and party enhancers include lava lamps; mood lights; spotlights; bubble machines; snow, fog, and haze machines; and mock flame machines.

Other props to consider are snowglobes, New Year's luminarias (white bags with fringe at the top to look like fireworks), mirrors (perhaps used on tabletops underneath candles), martini and champagne glasses filled with floating candles, colored marbles, flowers, party favors, or as candy dishes, wine, beer, and champagne bottles painted festive colors.

## New Year's Eve Party Themes

In addition to the various decorating motifs, you could incorporate overall themes in your party to tie in many elements—decor, menu, invitations, activities, favors, and so on. Some possible New Year's–related themes are:

## When the Clock Strikes 12

This theme can incorporate anything you can think of relating to time, dates, days, weeks, months, years, clocks, calendars, hourglasses, and midnight. Your invitation could feature a clock or a calendar page. Activities might include having guests come dressed as someone or something from their favorite era or year or holiday of the year. Centerpieces and other decorations can feature clocks in all forms (grandfather clocks, bell towers, and watches). You could have a round cake for dessert that is decorated to look like a clock.

For party favors, you could give out calendars or date books. A music lineup might feature songs that include the words *time*, *year*, *date*, *midnight*, *day*, or *month*, such as Frank Sinatra's "It Was a Very Good Year" and Cyndi Lauper's "Time After Time." Or include songs that actually have to do with time, such as "It's Now or Never." You could also include a game in which everyone has to list as many songs as they can think of with the above-mentioned words in them. It would be fun to see what people come up with.

## Lucky Charms

Because in the Italian tradition, New Year's Eve has a lot to do with ensuring good luck for the new year, you could incorporate a "lucky charms" theme. Have guests bring their favorite good luck charm. Feature lots of props and decorations relating to typical good luck charms such as horseshoes or ladybugs. You can also incorporate Italian good luck symbols such as the Italian horn or the Roman goddess of luck, Fortuna, who is the Roman New Year's good luck symbol. Hang garlic, mistletoe, and holly on the doors. Italian for "good luck" is *buona fortuna*.

## Roman Royalty

Another theme might be an extravagant "Roman royalty" party with chalices, long tables with decadent food, royal thrones, velvet, and Roman decor—black wrought iron, archways, tassels, bronze, columns, chariots, armor, amulets, swords, gladiators, gazing balls, and ornate structures.

You could have guests come dressed as their favorite royal of the Roman era or in their fanciest clothing, and serve very festive food and drinks. The invitation could be on a scroll. Replicas of Roman artwork, statues, sculptures, and icons might be used as decorations.

## New Year's Eve Party Activities and Touches

Whether or not you have a specific theme or decorate in a particular motif, a New Year's Eve party is bound to be a great time. All you need is a location, the right people, places for them to sit and stand comfortably, and enough for them to eat and drink. Everything else only adds more intensity to the fun. Here are some suggestions:

- Include a variety of lively and upbeat music, as well as a place to dance.
- Offer guests fun New Year's props, such as festive hats, horns and other noisemakers as well as confetti, streamers, bubbles, Silly String, and sparklers.
- Place banners, fun signs, wacky props, and helium balloons throughout the space.
- Arrange for a balloon drop at midnight.
- Set up stations with games for people to play—cards, Bingo, Tombola, Bunko, board games, charades, Pictionary, Trivial Pursuit, and others, including carnival-type games such as a ball or coin toss.
- Hire a palm reader or cartoonist.
- Make Italian-themed charms for drink glasses and let each one be different so guests can easily identify their drinks if they put them down. You can make charms out of just about anything, such as old earrings, little toys, party favors, clay, Monopoly pieces, candies, miniature Christmas tree ornaments, beads, or shells. Simply secure them to the stems of glasses with thin, pliable wire (found at craft stores).

- Include festive ice sculptures at buffet tables and serve drinks with ice cubes that have cranberries or mint leaves frozen in them.

- Encourage guests to share their New Year's resolutions, either by going around the table and saying them out loud, or by writing them down and then allowing one person to collect them and read them aloud. Prepare a special toast, and then encourage guests to add toasts and end them with "*Salude*" (the Italian toast).

## Italian Fortune or Proverb Eggs

Use hollowed-out egg shells decorated according to your theme. Make one for each guest. Put the eggs in a bowl and let each person choose one. Or, put one at each place setting (you could even personalize them with the person's name on the egg and a personalized message inside). At midnight, guests crack open the eggs to get their messages. You could also make a game out of this, and include a lottery number inside each egg. The person who gets the right number wins a prize (in honor of the Italian "fat ox" tradition, a lottery held in parts of Italy on New Year's Eve in which the winner gets to keep an ox adorned with flowers and ribbons). You might also put a fortune, an Italian proverb, a resolution, or whatever you choose in each egg.

# New Year's Gifts and Favors

In Italy, honey is given as a present at New Year's so that the coming year will be "as sweet as honey." Using honey and other Italian New Year's good luck symbols—bay leaves, laurel leaves, lentils, nuts, raisins, and coins—prepare gifts for guests to take home. Assemble little gift baskets that include little honey bears, bags of beans, a recipe for lentil soup, bay leaves in spice jars, and a note wishing guests a sweet and prosperous year. Or put together a basket, bag, or box of candy versions of these items—for example, candy mint lentils, Raisinets, and Bit O'Honey.

Give guests gold-wrapped chocolate coins in little tulle bags tied with ribbon, or a pot with seeds or a plant bulb to represent new life and growth for the new year. You could also put together little goodie bags filled with symbols related to the previous year or hopes for the new one (perhaps play money, toy baby bottles, cars, and planes). Or fill them with silly items like children's party favors, or with luxury items like mini bottles of champagne, champagne bubble bath, and so on. Or when your guests walk in the door you could give them party bags filled with party hats, streamers, confetti, noisemakers, game items, and even their cocktail napkin and drinking glass for the evening.

Take Polaroids and slip them into a souvenir card for guests to take home. The card could feature the year and a glittery cocktail glass or something that coordinates with your theme—and maybe a magnet on the back so they can put the card on their refrigerator at home.

## New Year's Menu

If you plan to have a family-style sit-down dinner for New Year's Eve, you might consider serving some of the traditional Italian dishes, such as *zampone* (pig leg), Italian sausage, lentils, and foods that contain nuts, raisins, beans, and honey. There are many ways to vary this meal, such as instead of *zampone*, serve some other form of pork—grilled pork chops, pork marsala, or pork roast served with baked or roasted potatoes—and a bean soup or salad. Or you could have Italian sausage with spaghetti and garlic bread with bean soup or salad.

Another option is a decadent meal of steak and lobster with clarified butter, and an appetizer of shrimp cocktail. Between the appetizer and the main meal, provide dinner guests with bowls of hot water or hot steamed cloths to clean their hands. Add lemon wedges, parsley sprigs, etched radishes, and other garnishes to the plates.

For a New Year's Eve party, consider serving appetizers and finger foods on buffet tables and circulating trays so guests can nibble as they mingle and sip cocktails. Many hors d'oeuvres can be picked up with fingers or toothpicks, while others require small plates and forks. Some ideas are pizza balls, made with pizza dough, cheese, and pepperoni and rolled into little balls; stuffed mushrooms; smoked salmon and cream cheese on mini toast pieces; sliced baguette bread with a variety of toppings (cheese spreads, bean dips, tomato-and-basil mixture, and crab dip); different kinds of canapes (crackers, pita pieces, puff pastries, and other breads, all smeared with different spreads); mini sandwiches; vegetables (carrot sticks, broccoli, cauliflower, radishes, celery); chilled crab; shrimp and lobster pieces with cocktail sauce for dipping; seared ahi tuna; stuffed potato skins; twice-baked potatoes; chicken wings; chicken fingers; chicken kabobs; bread bowls filled with dips and bread pieces for dipping; roasted garlic bulbs served on baguette slices; bruschetta; fondue; or festive rolled-up sandwiches on different types of bread each containing different fillings—such as smoked salmon and cucumber with a spicy mayonaise dressing, or cream cheese with nuts and spices, as well as tuna, chicken or egg salad, and prosciutto and provolone.

You could also arrange an elaborate antipasto including prosciutto-wrapped pears, mozzarella balls marinated in basil and olive oil; peppers; olives; an assortment of meats and cheeses; and pickled items. Or, set up individual mini platters or bowls. You can even make individual bowls out of hollowed-out bell peppers or tomatoes and fill them with various snacks such as olives, artichoke hearts, or cubes of mozzarella cheese, salami, and prosciutto.

On a dessert table, include various Italian cookies, pastries, candies, fruit dipped in chocolate (especially cherries, banana slices, strawberries, and bunches of grapes), and sparkling Jell-O.

No Italian New Year's Eve celebration is complete without champagne, specifically Italy's sparkling wine, Asti Spumante. Garnish champagne glasses with different types of fruit—grapes, lemon or orange wedges, cherries, pineapple chunks, strawberries, or cranberries. Or, adorn glasses with skewers loaded with several types of fruit.

Give champagne a twist by mixing it with various things, like peach or raspberry schnapps (one part schnapps to three parts champagne), or, for a dash of color and subtle flavor, add a splash of grape juice, cranberry juice, orange juice, or fruit punch. Make champagne cocktails. One version calls for soaking two sugar cubes in different liquors (maybe one in brandy and the other in Sweet and Sour mix), dropping the soaked sugar cubes into a champagne glass, and adding a drop of orange juice. Pour ice-cold champagne over the sugar cubes and the juice.

Or mix champagne with brandy, Burgundy wine, and sugar, or with cognac, cherry liqueur, lemon juice, and triple sec to make a champagne punch.

## New Year's Recipes

### Eggplant Parmesan Nuggets

1 whole eggplant
1 cup flour
¼ cup Parmesan cheese
½ teaspoon basil
¼ teaspoon salt

⅛ teaspoon pepper
2 eggs, beaten
2 tablespoons olive oil
2 cloves garlic, minced

Cut eggplant into bite-size pieces. Mix together flour, Parmesan cheese, basil, salt, and pepper. Dip eggplant pieces into beaten egg, then into flour mixture to coat. Heat oil in skillet and add garlic. Fry eggplant pieces until golden brown all over. Preheat oven to 350 degrees. Spray a cookie sheet with nonstick cooking spray and scatter eggplant pieces on sheet. Bake about 15 minutes. Serve as finger food on toothpicks with a marinara sauce for dipping, or over pasta for an entree.

# Italian Crab Cakes

4 tablespoons olive oil
1 whole white onion, finely chopped
3 to 4 cloves garlic, finely chopped
1 pound (canned) white crab meat
3 eggs, beaten
½ cup Parmesan cheese
1 cup Italian-style bread crumbs

2 tablespoons Italian salad dressing
1 tablespoon Italian seasoning mix
   (basil, thyme, rosemary, marjoram, minced garlic)
½ teaspoon salt
⅛ teaspoon pepper
½ cup white wine

Heat 2 tablespoons of olive oil in skillet. Add onion and garlic and cook about 5 minutes. Place sautéed onion and garlic in large glass bowl and allow to cool (about 10 minutes). In a bowl, mix together crabmeat, eggs, Parmesan cheese, bread crumbs, salad dressing, seasoning, salt, and pepper. Form crab mixture into patties of desired size. Heat 2 tablespoons oil in skillet, add wine, and heat until simmering. Cook crab patties in oil and wine until lightly browned on both sides. Serve with tomato-based sauce, cocktail sauce, horseradish, or ranch dressing. You can also add a slice of mozzarella cheese to each crab cake and bake until cheese melts. Serve on a plate on top of marinara sauce.

# Italian Lettuce Wraps

2 whole tomatoes, chopped
½ cup mushrooms, chopped
1 whole white onion, chopped
¼ cup black olives, chopped
1 bell pepper, chopped

1 tablespoon olive oil
1 tablespoon balsamic vinegar
Salt and pepper to taste
12 large leaves of lettuce

Mix tomatoes, mushrooms, onion, olives, and pepper with olive oil, vinegar, salt, and pepper. Spoon mixture onto lettuce pieces. Roll and secure with toothpicks. (You can also add artichoke hearts, chickpeas, shredded mozzarella cheese, and grated Parmesan to the stuffing mixture, if desired.)

# Italian Piggy Pockets

1 package of ready-made pizza
    dough

1 pound precooked Italian sausage,
    cut into ½-inch slices

Roll out dough and cut into 2-inch squares. Place sausage pieces in centers of dough squares and fold dough around them, pinching edges shut. Bake for about 20 minutes in a 350-degree oven (or according to directions on dough package). Serve with toothpicks and dipping sauce of choice.

# Fried Mozzarella

2 pounds mozzarella, cut into strips
    about ½-inch thick
2 cups flour

4 eggs, beaten
2 cups seasoned bread crumbs
4 tablespoons oil (olive or vegetable)

Coat mozzarella in flour. Dip in egg and then coat in bread crumbs. Heat oil in pan. Brown mozzarella on each side. Make sure not to burn—they cook quickly. Serve immediately with tomato sauce for dipping.

# Ham Roll-Ups

1 (8-ounce) package cream cheese,
    at room temperature
1 tablespoon sour cream
1 tablespoon dry white wine
1 tablespoon Parmesan cheese
1 red bell pepper, finely chopped

1 white onion, finely chopped
½ cup almonds or pecans, finely
    chopped
½ teaspoon black pepper
1 tablespoon basil
1 pound deli ham, sliced

Mix cream cheese, sour cream, wine, Parmesan cheese, bell pepper, onion, nuts, black pepper, and basil. Stack two slices of ham (thick enough to hold mixture) and spread mixture on top. Roll and secure with toothpicks. Cut into equal-size pieces.

# Mini Salmon Sandwiches

1 (8-ounce) package cream cheese
1 tablespoon sour cream
½ cup celery, chopped
½ cup onion (white or green),
    chopped

12 slices white bread, crusts cut off
2 carrots, shredded
6 thin slices smoked salmon
2 large (or 4 medium) tomatoes, very
    thinly sliced

Mix together cream cheese, sour cream, celery, and onion. Spread 6 slices of bread with this mixture. Top each with carrot shavings, salmon, and a tomato slice. Close sandwiches with the remaining bread slices. Cut each sandwich diagonally into quarters and secure with toothpicks.

# Uncle Vic's Gnocchi
## (Potato Dumplings)

1¾ cups sifted four

3 medium potatoes (about 1 pound),
    mashed

Make a well in the center of the flour. Add mashed potatoes (they should be added when they are very hot). Mix well to make a soft, elastic dough. Turn dough onto a lightly floured surface and knead.

Break off small pieces of dough and roll pieces to pencil thickness—cut into pieces about ¾-inch long. Curl each piece by pressing lightly with index finger and pulling the piece of dough toward you. Gnocchi may also be shaped by rolling each piece lightly off a lowered fork. Bring 3 quarts of water to a boil in a saucepan. Gradually add gnocchi. Boil rapidly about 10 minutes, or until tender. Drain.

# Claro's Veal Cutlets With Mushrooms
## and Marsala Wine

¼ cup butter
½ cup olive oil
8 veal cutlets
Flour for dredging veal
1 small onion, chopped

2 to 3 cloves garlic, minced
½ pound fresh mushrooms, cleaned
    and sliced
1 cup dry marsala wine
Salt and pepper to taste

Preheat oven to 350 degrees. In a large frying pan, heat butter and oil to medium hot. Dredge veal cutlets in flour, shaking off excess. Fry cutlets until golden brown on both sides. Transfer to an ovenproof dish. Add onion, garlic, and mushrooms to the same frying pan and sautée for about 5 minutes. Add marsala wine and cook for another few minutes. Add salt and pepper. Pour mixture over cutlets in dish. Bake for 15 to 20 minutes.

## Claro's Veal Cutlets in Lemon Sauce

1 pound Italian-style veal cutlets
Flour, seasoned with salt and
    pepper (enough to coat cutlets)
3 tablespoons olive oil

3 tablespoons butter
½ cup fresh lemon juice
2 tablespoons minced parsley

Dip veal cutlets into flour mixture. Heat oil and butter in a large skillet. Brown meat on both sides and set aside. Pour off a little of the excess oil. Add lemon juice and parsley to remaining oil in skillet. Blend well. Add veal and stir well to coat thoroughly with parsley and lemon juice. Cover pan and simmer about 15 minutes. Garnish with fresh parsley and lemon slices.

## Claro's Risotto with Peas

3 cups chicken broth (This is an
    approximate amount; you may
    use a little more or less until the
    risotto is cooked the way you like
    it. You can use either canned
    broth or bouillon.)
2 tablespoons butter
2 tablespoons olive oil
1 medium onion

1 tablespoon garlic, chopped
1 pound uncooked aborio rice
1 cup dry white wine
½ teaspoon powdered saffron
1 pound frozen peas
Salt and pepper to taste
Grated Romano cheese
½ pound fontina cheese, grated
    (optional)

Prepare chicken broth and set aside. In large, heavy-bottomed saucepan, sauté butter, olive oil, onion, and garlic until onions are clear but not brown. Add rice and stir until well coated. (You might need to add a little more olive oil.) Add wine and stir well. Begin adding chicken broth a few ladles at a time, stirring frequently, until absorbed. After adding most of broth, taste the rice. It should be cooked through but firm, not mushy. Add the saffron to the last ladle of broth. Stir and add to the risotto. This step will give the risotto a sort of golden color. Add the frozen peas and stir. (Any cooked vegetable could also be added at this point.) Add salt, pepper, grated Romano, and fontina (if desired). Stir well and serve with a little grated cheese on top.

# Claro's Sausage With Peppers, Onions, and Wine

2 pounds fresh Italian sausage
2 tablespoons olive oil
1 red bell pepper, coarsely chopped
1 green bell pepper, coarsely
   chopped

1 white onion, coarsely chopped
¼ cup dry white wine

Cut sausages into single links. Do not poke holes into sausage casings. Brown sausages in skillet in olive oil over medium-high heat, stirring often with a wooden spoon, until they are about halfway cooked. Add peppers, onion, and wine. Continue to cook another 30 to 45 minutes until sausages are done. (Prepare in the oven using the same ingredients. Combine all ingredients together in a glass baking dish. Preheat oven to 350 degrees and bake uncovered for about 1 hour, stirring every so often with a wooden spoon.)

*11*

# St. Joseph's Day

SPRING BRINGS WITH IT a whole new season of celebrations. St. Joseph's Day, March 19, is a major holiday for Italian-Americans. To celebrate, many prepare an abundance of meatless foods (because it falls in Lent), including the popular zeppole pastry, *sfinci*, and breads made in dozens of different shapes that adorn an altar built in the saint's honor.

St. Joseph's Day, also known as Festa de San Giuseppe, is a feast of thanks and is widely celebrated by Italians and Italian-Americans alike. It is perhaps the most widely recognized saint's feast day, especially by Sicilians.

This feast features elaborate altars, called "St. Joseph Tables," that are decorated festively and covered with food. People come together—in private and public celebrations—for a blessing, devotional prayer, and to share in the feast.

## Who Was St. Joseph?

St. Joseph is the patron saint of many things, including family life, fathers, Sicily, carpenters, hand labor, workers, the universal church, social justice, cart makers, unwed mothers, orphans, and dying (or a happy death). Joseph took on the roles of husband to Mary and earthly father to Jesus.

He served as a devoted husband and father. He was a humble, compassionate, caring, and just man who was obedient to God. According to the Catholic Church, he has always been regarded as the family protector, the guardian of the spiritual home, and the prime example of fathers. He was the one man whom God trusted to raise His own son. It is said that St. Joseph is the patron saint of the dying because he died with Jesus and Mary by his side, the way most people would prefer to leave this earth.

## The History and Background of St. Joseph's Day

In the Middle Ages, there was a severe and devastating drought in Sicily that caused famine, suffering, and starvation. The people prayed to St. Joseph to help put an end to this suffering; if he did, they promised, they would thank him with a great feast. St. Joseph answered their prayers, brought rain, and ended their dire state. The people kept their promise and prepared an enormous feast in his honor. Farmers brought produce, bakers brought baked goods, and everyone pitched in to set up huge community banquet tables. Everyone was invited to come and enjoy the feast, including the poor and needy.

## St. Joseph's Day in Italy

From then on, huge Thanksgiving-type celebrations have taken place every year on St. Joseph's feast day. The holiday is also considered the Italian Father's Day and/or Thanksgiving, and it can last for up to three days. In Sicily, where the feast day began, the celebrations are the most festive, with massive street parades and gatherings. Prior to the feast day, people build elaborate altars and prepare large quantities of food to share with the community. St. Joseph's Day usually starts with a mass, followed by a procession through town to the huge banquet, which is often in the town square. The parade is led by a Holy Family (Mary, Joseph, and

Jesus), portrayed by different townspeople. Also on this day, people spend time in prayer (especially to thank the saint for helping their prayers get answered) and strive to be kind and giving to others, as well as give to the poor in St. Joseph's name.

## St. Joseph's Day Celebrations

Many Italians and Italian-Americans hold open houses, where anyone can come and eat (family, friends, and people in need). And while there are several public St. Joseph's Day celebrations—usually taking place at Catholic churches—there are many private versions that take place in individual homes or neighborhoods.

Sometimes an entire room is transformed into a sanctuary devoted to St. Joseph, with an altar covered with food and beautiful decorations as well as latticework adorned with greenery, ribbons, myrtle branches, bay leaves, oranges, lemons, and small decorative breads.

Oftentimes people will hang olive branches, palm fronds, or other kinds of branches and greenery over their front doors to let others know that a St. Joseph celebration is taking place inside and that they are welcome to participate.

In some neighborhoods, children are chosen to dress as the Holy Family, and as angels and other saints. After mass, the Holy Family walks around the neighborhood in a procession, knocking on three different doors (which are planned ahead of time). At the first two houses, the homeowner asks who is there, and the kids reply: "A weary family looking for a place to rest." The reply is, "Go away. We have no room here." At the third house, the children knock, the owners ask who's there, and the kids reply, "The Holy Family looking for a place to stay." The owners, who are the hosts at the house where the table is set up and the feast will take place, say something like, "Enter. There is always room in our hearts and homes for the Holy Family." The Holy Family is seated at a special table and served first.

The purpose of the celebration is for people to share their blessings with those in need, whether that means close family and friends or large groups—church congregations, neighborhoods, or entire towns. On this day, people honor and pray to St. Joseph throughout the evening, with such prayers as "May St. Joseph always look down on us and guide us through our daily lives."

## The St. Joseph Table

The centerpiece of the St. Joseph's Day celebration is the altar, or St. Joseph Table. It is built as a ritual to thank St. Joseph for recovering from an illness, avoiding an accident, or the saint's protecting a loved one from harm. There are many variations of the table. Many are built with three levels, or tiers, representing the Holy Trinity.

Sometimes the table is arranged in the shape of a cross. It is draped in fine white linen and covered with flowers. On the top tier is a statue of St. Joseph. Other items on the table include food and other signs of bounty, symbols of St. Joseph such as sandals and lilies, votive candles, sweets, cakes, oranges, lemons, breads, fruit, and vegetables. Ribbon streamers are sometimes hung from columns to which people pin money to donate to the poor (or a certain charity). Long ago, it was customary to beg for the supplies to build the altar.

A Catholic priest often blesses the altar and the food around it, and the blessed bread is distributed and eaten. It is said that eating a piece of the blessed bread brings good fortune.

Foods on the table include braided breads (called *cucadati* or *cud-ureddi*) formed and decorated in a variety of symbolic shapes, such as a cross, crown (for Jesus), staff (for Joseph), palm (for Mary), and smaller breads (*rastedde*). The decorative breads are formed in almost every shape in nature as well as Christian symbols and representations of St. Joseph. Some of the shapes include instruments of the Passion of Christ; suns, moons and stars; flowers and birds; peacocks (to represent the glory of man); Christian symbols like monstrances and spada (which hold the sacred Host), chalices (for the consecration of the bread and wine at the Last Supper), and the Cross (for the crucifixion); hearts (which represent Christ); doves; baskets; fish; shellfish; St. Joseph's staff; carpenter tools like nails, hammers, saws, and ladders; scepters; and beards. Other breads include *panini* and cucidatti (huge devotional rounds).

There is often also a devotional altar, either on the St. Joseph Table or on a separate table, with a statue of the saint holding the Baby Jesus. This table serves as a place for people to dedicate special prayers for loved ones in need and for those who have passed away. The prayers are often written on a piece of paper and put in baskets on the table in the hope that St. Joseph will intervene and help get their prayers answered.

Much as they did during the drought in Sicily long ago, people make promises that if their prayers are answered (for restored health, employment, or other blessings) the recipient will honor St. Joseph on his feast day.

## St. Joseph's Day Feast Foods

The food is simple and signifies poverty, and is sometimes referred to as a "poor man's meal." Because St. Joseph's Day falls in the season of Lent, none of the foods contain meat.

The feast often starts with a St. Joseph–style minestrone, called *minestra di San Guise* (meaning "confusion" or "chaos"), which uses all kinds of vegetables—whatever the cook has on hand. No cheese is eaten during this time, so instead of Parmesan, dry toasted bread crumbs are sprinkled on the soup.

Other dishes include *cuscusu* (couscous); a "dry" spaghetti served with bread crumbs, raisins, and walnuts; *cavazune* (pronounced "gava-june"), a pasta shaped like huge ravioli that is three inches long, stuffed with a filling of chickpeas sweetened with sugar and molasses, and then deep fried in olive oil; *pasta can sarde* (a tomato-based dish with the slightly sweet flavor of fennel); fava beans; *pesce d'uova* (a mixture of bread crumbs, garlic, and parsley); *arancini* (rice croquettes the size of tennis balls with a filling of fresh spring peas and tomato sauce); olive sauce; pasta Milanese; pasta with *mollica*; pasta with *legume*; and frittatas (omelets) of all kinds.

There is an abundance of fruit filling trays and wicker baskets. Oranges, lemons, fat pears, thorny prickly pears, grapes, and apples are just a few.

Vegetable dishes are abundant and include fried or stuffed cauliflower, artichokes, *pesci di funghi* (mushrooms dipped in egg and bread crumbs, then fried), zucchini, eggplant, cardoons, asparagus, peas, peppers, and artichoke stuffed with bread crumbs, Parmesan cheese, basil, and wine.

Several fish courses include *baccala*; deep-fried smelts; fried eels; spaghetti with anchovies; fried cod with tomato; *sarde fritte come sogliole* (sardines fried like sole, marinated in vinegar, then dipped in flour); *calamari riponi* (fried calamari stuffed with garlic, bread crumbs, and parsley); *crocchette di merluzzo fresco bollito* (fried croquettes of fresh cod mixed with *besciamella* [a butter nutmeg sauce], Parmesan cheese, and fresh parsley); *baccala fritto* (bite-size pieces of fried *baccala*); and *gamberetti fritti* (fried shrimp with fine slices of lemon).

The breads, in addition to the decorative ones in the many shapes already mentioned, include large round loaves, breads wrapped around dyed eggs (dough babies), and St. Joseph's Bread (a crusty yeast bread).

Sweets are also abundant, as St. Joseph is also the patron saint of pastry cooks. They include zeppole, or *zeppoli di San Giuseppe* (a deep-fried pastry), the traditional sweet the Neapolitans have always made to celebrate St. Joseph's Day; *sfinge* (also called *sfinci*, *sfinge de san Giuiseppe*, and *sfinghi*), a light, moist fritter or doughnut with a ricotta cheese basis (which is made by dropping a teaspoon of batter into hot oil, and then sprinkling it with powdered sugar and sometimes cinnamon); *persiche* (Sicilian cream-filled pastries made to look like peaches); *cassadini* (sweet ravioli); *strufoli* (fried honey dough balls); cakes in different shapes (such as a lamb or a Bible); cannoli; anise slices; *cassata*; *tetu*; *pignolata*; *caponatina*; *cassetedde*; panettone; candy; cookies; *pignolatti* (a pineconelike cluster or mound made up of many fried pastry pieces all glazed with honey brittle); and biscotti.

# St. Joseph's Day Celebration Stories
## From Italian-Americans

### Josie Vinci

"The celebrations took place in someone's home, where the altar was created in the dining room, on the dining room table—they would build the altar out of plywood and cover it with a tablecloth, candles, and flowers.

"Everyone in our family participated. The night before we said the rosary, and on St. Joseph's Day a priest came over at eleven A.M. and did a blessing of the table. There would be a procession and people dressed up to play the Blessed Mother, Joseph, Jesus, St. Anne, and other saints. People who were ill or in need of a blessing were sometimes the ones who dressed up. They would go to three neighbors' homes and ask, 'Do you have room for me and my family?' and they would be turned away. Then they would go to the home where the celebration was (usually my mom's) and ask if they could stay. There they would be told, 'Yes, of course I have room.' Then Mom served them first and they had to taste everything (there was whole salmon, pasta, and sauce). There was a basket and envelopes, and people would put money either in envelopes in the basket or just in the basket; however much they wanted. People brought over baked goods, flowers, rings of bread, bananas, oranges, apples, and candles with the saints' pictures on them."

### Dorothy Pantleo

"The idea of the St. Joseph's Day Table was a promise to do work and sacrifice time in exchange for a blessing for someone in need. People would come and we would feed them. The tables were offered for the blind center or an orphanage. There was no meat; there was wheat, wine, fruit, vegetables, cookies, cakes, and breads in many shapes—cross, saw, nail, cane, ring; things that represented St. Joseph. It was a French/Italian bread.

# St. Joseph's Day, Food, and Customs

*Professor Philip J. Di Novo*

"March 19 marks the feast of St. Joseph. For Italians, it is a religious and ethnic celebration. It is a day we honor St. Joseph, the foster father of Jesus and the husband of Mary. It is a day that marks our people's being sent rain during a severe drought when many people were dying of starvation, and a day we keep a promise made by our ancestors for saving our people from certain death. On St. Joseph's Day we share with the needy, an important Christian obligation. All these reasons make the celebration special. Because of the love of God and St. Joseph's intercession, we have many reasons for holding the celebration.

"Many kinds of vegetable *minestras*, very thick soups, are prepared and served at this celebration, but no cheese is eaten on St. Joseph's Day. This is to remind us that our people were too poor to have cheese.

"Lentils, favas, and all types of dried beans are cooked and served with escarole and other leafy vegetables. Pasta *can le sarde* (spaghetti with sardines and fennel), fresh sardines, double layers of stuffed sardines, chunks of fresh chilled fennel, large black oil-cured olives, fried artichoke hearts, stuffed baked escarole rolls, fried cauliflower rosettes, spinach and asparagus *frosce* [omelets], braided bread wreaths, large navel oranges, and pomegranates are all part of La Tavola di San Giuseppe, a meatless feast table, prepared and shared with those in need.

"My mother hosted the St. Joseph's Day feast for fifteen years. My dad was sick and she promised St. Joseph she would do it until he got back on his feet and went to work. On top of the plywood table/altar was a statue of St. Joseph. People would leave stuff on the porch two weeks before—we never knew who left it."

## David Manzari

"Saint Joseph is my brother's namesake. We would always have the pastry zeppole, which is a fried or baked pastry dough, with cream and blueberry on top. In Italy, we celebrated Father's Day on St. Joseph's Day as well."

"A traditional Festa di San Giuseppe might start with chilled marsala lentil soup, spaghetti with finocchio and sardine sauce, roasted artichokes, escarole salad, St. Joseph's *sfinge*, amaretti, macaroons, roasted nuts, green almonds, fruit, espresso, and Benedictine or anisette. Intermittenly during the meal, *'Viva San Giuseppe!'* is shouted in tribute and admiration for this great saint. The special dessert, St. Joseph's *sfinge*, is made in many ways and is typically a large, round cream puff filled with ricotta and topped with red cherries and sections of glazed orange.

"Each region of Italy has its own unique food and desserts to mark the feast. In Abruzzi, people eat *covezun di San Giuseppe*, a tiny baked turnover of thinly rolled sweet dough filled with chopped walnuts and chocolate. Farther north, near Bologna, *sfrappole* are a March 19 specialty. *Sfrappole* are strips of sweet noodle dough that are knotted, fried, and sugared. In Tuscany, rice cakes are served. In Pappardella di San Giuseppe, traditionally cooked noodles or *ferretti* [spirals] tossed in olive oil with toasted walnuts, bread crumbs, and sugar is served. Zeppole originated in Calabria, and is a puff filled with cream, a cherry, and sections of glazed orange. In Sicily, Pane di San Giuseppe, a rich sweet bread, is the centerpiece for the feast. The beautiful table also has a statue of St. Joseph and the Christ Child, flowers, and candles. A symbolic dish of uncooked fava beans is set on the table to represent the legendary famine's only available food."

## Mary Fanara

"On St. Joseph's Day, we made dishes and put them on the big altars. Everyone contributed. Mom made up huge amounts of breads every year. It was a community thing—they decorated the altar and displayed it for several days, and on St. Joseph's Day, everyone ate the food."

## Mary Linda Daddona

"On St. Joseph's Day, tables are adorned with food, including zeppole, a pastry filled with custard. We make the bread in different shapes—crosses, canes, and so on. It's an egg bread that is braided with sesame seeds. Nobody's supposed to go hungry on St. Joseph's Day."

# Ideas for Celebrating St. Joseph's Day

Whether or not your family, neighborhood, community, or church celebrates St. Joseph's Day with the table, procession, Holy Family knocking on three doors, or traditional foods, you can pay tribute to the charitable saint in many ways. If you don't already put on or participate in putting on a St. Joseph's Day feast, perhaps you might want to consider it.

On a small scale, you might prepare a meal for your family that includes some of the customary foods—such as minestrone, a seafood dish, fried vegetables and bread, followed by a dessert of zeppole or *sfinge* (you can find them at Italian markets and bakeries at that time of year).

You might acquire a small statue or picture of St. Joseph and create a small altar—on a side table, shelf, or even as your dining table centerpiece for that meal—and display it along with a basket of fruit and bread, some flowers, a rosary, and any other items you choose.

For a more traditional celebration, you might set up a special table and devote it to the saint. In addition to the statue or picture, flowers, and fruit, display the feast day foods, including some decorative breads in different shapes. As is customary during these celebrations, you might call upon others to prepare certain dishes.

Hold an open house for people to come and visit, eat a variety of feast foods, pray, write down petitions and place them in a special basket, and donate money to a charity. Perhaps you could include a ribbon or streamer for them to pin money to or a jar or basket with envelopes for people to donate as much as they wish. Then donate the money to a charity (such as a disabled children's organization, the Red Cross, a cancer or other illness society, or a church charity).

For the altar, consider erecting a folding table in a separate room, such as a guest room or formal living room. That room will become a sanctuary to the saint. Or use a coffee table, end table, dining room table or server, countertop, desktop, or shelf.

For decorating, you might use fine linens, statuary, candles, crystal or silver candleholders, candelabra, flowers, vases, baskets, serving trays, framed photos (such as of deceased loved ones you want to pray for), water fountains, ribbons, streamers, branches, greenery, and backdrops such as lattice, fabric, or bulletin boards on which to pin pictures and dedications to St. Joseph.

Choose three children to dress as Jesus, Mary, and Joseph, and others to dress as angels and saints of their choice. If two neighbors are willing to participate, have the kids knock on two doors "looking for shelter" and get turned away. At your home, invite them in and have them sit down for a meal. Or, rather than having the children walk around the neighborhood, you could have them knock at three different doors within your house.

Further involve children in the celebration by having them learn more about St. Joseph. Have children write an essay and/or draw a picture (depending on their ages) of the saint, and then feature their work on the altar. Children can also write and draw on a large banner that may be hung above the table. Ask children to write or tell how their dad is like St. Joseph.

More ways to celebrate St. Joseph's Day:

- Honor your dad with a second Father's Day. Give him cards, gifts, thanks, and love.

- Become a foster parent, big brother or sister, or volunteer at a youth center or children's hospital.

- Hold a raffle, sale, or auction on food items at your St. Joseph's Day celebration and donate the money to a charity.

# Recipes

## Claro's Sfingi (Fried Dough)

1 pound fresh pizza dough
½ cup raisins
Salad oil for frying

Granulated sugar for coating
1 teaspoon ground cinnamon

Knead dough well, mixing in raisins. Let rise in covered bowl until dough doubles in size. Heat salad oil in medium-size saucepan. Fry small pieces of dough until golden brown. Drain on paper towels. Place sugar and cinnamon in bag and shake warm fried dough in it.

## St. Joseph's Day Zeppoli

½ cup butter
1 tablespoon sugar
½ teaspoon salt
1 cup hot water
1 cup flour, sifted

4 eggs
1 teaspoon orange peel, grated
1 teaspoon lemon peel, grated
Whipped cream, either ready-made
    or fresh

Mix butter, sugar, salt, and hot water in saucepan and bring to boil. Add flour and stir until mixture forms a smooth ball (about 3 minutes). Remove from heat. Beat in eggs, 1 at a time. Beat until smooth. Add orange and lemon peel, and mix. On a lightly greased baking sheet, drop tablespoonfuls of dough. Bake at 450 degrees about 15 minutes. Lower heat to 350 degrees and bake for an additional 15 to 20 minutes, or until golden. Remove to rack and cool. Cut a slit in one side of each pastry and fill with whipped cream.

# Linguine and Clam Sauce

3 cups tomatoes, chopped
¼ cup water
2 cloves garlic, sliced
1 tablespoon parsley
1 teaspoon salt
½ teaspoon pepper

½ teaspoon oregano
1 tablespoon basil
½ cup white wine
2 cups canned little neck clams,
    with juice
1 pound package linguine, prepared

In a saucepan, mix together tomatoes, water, garlic, parsley, salt, pepper, oregano, and basil, and simmer about 10 minutes. Add wine and simmer about 1 minute. Add clam juice, mix, and simmer 10 minutes. Add clams and simmer until heated through. Serve over linguine.

# *12*

# *Italian-American Easter Traditions*

THE EASTER SEASON is an important and highly celebrated time for Italian-Americans, with many religious rituals, seasonal activities, and a period of fasting that ends with an enormous feast. It is the Christmas season of the spring, beginning with several spiritual holidays—Ash Wednesday, Palm Sunday, Holy Thursday, Good Friday, and Holy Saturday—on which mass is attended, and an entire season of Lent, during which Catholics abstain from eating meat on Fridays and are expected to temporarily sacrifice a chosen pleasure—to give up chocolate, sodas, sweets, shopping, or what have you.

Easter Sunday, when the fasting ends and the celebration begins, is the highlight of the season. Most Italian-Americans spend Easter Sunday by attending mass in the morning and then having one or two feasts—any combination of breakfast, brunch, lunch, and dinner. A variety of traditional foods is consumed. These foods often include a number of egg dishes (from hard-boiled eggs to frittatas), lamb, goat or pig, potatoes or pasta, salads, vegetables, and an assortment of festive holiday breads and desserts. Of course, the meal includes wine, and dessert is served with coffee and liqueurs.

# Memories of Easter

The Easter season started on Ash Wednesday. Because I attended Catholic school, my entire class would go to mass that day, where the priest placed ashes on our foreheads. We were all encouraged to give up something for Lent—meaning it would be a sin to have that thing before Easter. From what I remember, I would usually make it something pretty specific, like ice cream or M&Ms, rather than sweets in general, so I knew that I could stick with it.

We also were not allowed to eat meat on Fridays during Lent. On those Fridays, my family often ate cheese pizza for dinner, and if we were lucky and our parents didn't have time to make our lunches, Dad would bring McDonald's Fillet O'Fish sandwiches and fries to school for us.

With my class, I attended mass on Holy Thursday, and a solemn service on Good Friday we did the Stations of the Cross, where we would go around the church praying in front of each individual image of Jesus' crucifixion. Good Friday was a somber day on which we were asked to reflect on Christ's death and what it meant to us as Catholics.

Then we would have a classroom Easter party, followed by an Easter egg hunt; depending on what grade we were in, we either helped hide the eggs or we hunted for them. Then we had the whole next week off for Easter vacation.

The Saturday before Easter, my family spent the day coloring eggs— lots of them. When we were very young, that night we would leave milk and carrots out for the Easter bunny.

On Easter morning we awoke to a trail of jelly beans leading from our bedrooms to the hidden Easter baskets (sometimes the trails misled us to dead ends, but the search was part of the fun; sometimes the jelly beans would be all sticky because the dogs had found them and licked them first). My mom put together the biggest, most elaborate Easter baskets. There would always be chocolate eggs and bunnies, Reese's peanut butter eggs, little fuzzy (fake) chicks, Slinkys, Silly Putty, and other toys and games.

Then we would go to church dressed up in our brand-new Easter outfits (as a little girl, my outfits usually consisted of a fancy fluffy dress, white patent, leather shoes, and lacy socks). Then we would come home and eat Easter breakfast, which included an egg-and-cheese casserole, bacon, sausage, hash browns, and toast.

Later the relatives all gathered at our house for the midday Easter feast. Both sets of grandparents also brought us Easter baskets; one would always have plastic eggs with money in them.

There was an Easter egg hunt for the kids, with all sorts of goodies hidden throughout the yard, including plastic eggs containing money, candy, and little toys, and a "golden egg." Whoever found this won five dollars (this amount went up over the years). My oldest cousin, Victor, almost always found it. Sometimes we would have egg fights with confetti eggs we had spent days preparing.

The Easter feast consisted of ham; turkey; potato casserole; green bean casserole; twisted Easter breads with colored eggs baked into them; antipasto plates with peppers, olives, and pickles; deviled eggs; and salads. For dessert there would be an assortment of cakes—often a strawberry shortcake was among them—pies, cookies, and candies.

## Easter Memories

### Judge Alfred J. DiBona Jr.

"My parents, Alfred and Catilda DiBona, were born in the United States. My ancestors were from the Abruzzi region of Italy. My grandfather returned to his native Italy when my father was two years old. Therefore, my father was raised and educated in Filignano, Italy, in the province of Isernia (then part of the province of Campobasso). He returned to America when he was nineteen years old in 1913, where he experienced entry through Ellis Island, and then settled in south Philadelphia, where he lived until he passed away on July 11, 1981. He was a hardworking husband, father, and grandfather of my two children, Alfred and Barbara.

"My mother was dedicated to her family but would not permit anyone to cook in her kitchen, and she was the best.

"My father did not cook except breakfast on Easter morning. My father's specialty was *la frittata*, an egg omelet stuffed with Italian sausage. He would get up at five A.M. and after church begin the preparations. He cooked and cut the five pounds of sausage into small pieces. Each omelet contained sixteen eggs. The result was a masterpiece of three omelets the size of a large platter and about four inches thick with a golden color. Breakfast was served at eight A.M. After my dad cut one of the omelets, we began to dig in. We all waited for Mom's critique. Her comments over the years varied: too much salt, not enough salt, too much sausage, not enough sausage. Only Mom made the comments while we listened and ate to our hearts' content. The memory of those special occasions will be with my family and me for generations to come."

## Jean A. DiBona

"My father, Pasquale DiBona, born in Philadelphia, Pennsylvania, went to Italy with his widowed mother. Their family lived in Filignano, Campobasso. My father was called to fight for the Italian army in World War I, and was a prisoner in Bosnia until the war ended. He returned to Filignano, married Regina DiBona (she had the same last name), and had their first two children, Helen and Louis. They all returned to Philadelphia, then along came Michael and Jean.

"Living in south Philadelphia, pre–World War II, was a great experience. The good times overshadowed the bad. We were a close family, and friends were just as close. My father was a tailor and taught us all the same.

"Holidays were always fun, lots of cooking to be sure. My favorite was our Holy Saturday noon meal. After Lent, the good polenta with sausage in tomato sauce was so special. My brother, Mike, and I would take turns stirring the polenta in a great big pot. We had to stand on a kitchen chair for that. Then Mom would spoon out the polenta in patties onto a large oval platter, at least three layers high, with the sausage, sauce, and cheese between the layers. There was always plenty, as we never knew how many visitors would just happen to be passing by with Easter greetings.

"I guess it was the way Mom had it timed, to have that big platter ready for the last cheese sprinkling over it just as the neighboring church bells would ring. Mom said they were ringing the bells to announce the ending of the fast/abstinence and time to rejoice. We would all gather around the table and give thanks, and enjoy!

"We missed the church bells ringing after we moved from south Philadelphia after the end of the war. Our immediate family still gathers for holiday dinners—Easter, Thanksgiving, and Christmas—even though we no longer live in the same places. Mom and Pop are no longer with us, and there have been many other changes. The Easter Sunday frittata is smaller, the carbonara has less bacon, but the polenta never comes close to the way Mom used to make it. I always say it is because the church bells are missing."

## Frances Gendimenico Kaufmann

"Good Friday was always the day my mother made her Easter pies. It was a solemn day in our normally bustling home. Six active and curious children had to try to be quiet, stay away from the TV, fast until dinner, and abstain from meat for two days. It was not easy. I always loved to watch my mother as she moved through our big kitchen lovingly creating six golden-crusted pies. The aromas of ham baking in the oven and sausage crackling on the stove tempted me to snatch just one little bite. But I knew I had to be good.

"The reward would come on Sunday morning with the first taste of a wonderful, rich combination of cheeses, eggs, ham, sausage, and fresh parsley. It was always worth the wait. My mother, Nancy, learned how to make Easter pie from her mother, Francesca Dorso, who arrived on Ellis Island from Centola, Italy, on Columbus Day 1905. I never tired of keeping Mom company as she rolled the dough, chopped and mixed the ingredients, and told me stories of her childhood. Little by little I was allowed to boil the eggs, chop the ham, and stir the filling in the gigantic mixing bowl. My mother can no longer make her Easter pies. So every year on Good Friday, our home in New Jersey is filled with the aromas I remember from Mom's kitchen. Instead of six pies, I make two. Everyone is watching their weight and their cholesterol levels these days. On Easter morning, Mom takes the first bite of my Easter pie, and I hold my breath. When I see her face light up with her sweet smile of approval, I am satisfied. The tradition continues for another year."

## Diane Reid

"Easter meals are a combination of American and Italian. We try to make Nanny's egg bread (three hard-boiled eggs braided in dough to represent the three Wise Men) and the cross with one hard-cooked egg in the middle."

## Joyce Spataro

"At Easter we always made colored eggs like everyone else. We had ham with all the trimmings, but always served some kind of macaroni. We make Easter pies that are filled with pepperoni, a white, soft cheese formed in a basket mold, also called *formagetto*, mozzarella cheese, Parmesan cheese, prosciutto, and eggs. We also make a rice pie that is filled with rice, ricotta, vanilla, eggs, and milk."

## David Manzari

"On Good Friday we don't eat meat. We have a big dinner the week before, on Palm Sunday. We celebrate Easter the following Sunday. My mother or father would use the palms we got from church the week before and a bottle of holy water to bless everyone at the table. We would eat an egg with an orange slice on top for an appetizer, and have Easter cake, which is a pastry with colored sprinkles and boiled egg inside, called *scarcella*. On Easter Monday—Little Easter, Pasquetta—we don't work, we go to church."

## Rina Mele

"On Palm Sunday we go to church and receive a palm. On Ash Wednesday we walk around with a cross of ash on our forehead. On Good Friday we don't eat meat. On Easter Sunday we wake up, attend morning mass, and have an Easter egg hunt. We have the family dinner, which consists of antipasto, lasagna, lamb baked in the oven, barbecued lamb, fried vegetables, ricotta calzone, espresso, and *lemoncello*, a popular Italian liqueur.

"Many traditions are celebrated in Italy and not here, such as on Good Friday in Italy, there is a parade. Here, on Easter Monday, we go to work; in Italy, we went out to the park and had a picnic."

## Mary Fanara

"Growing up in Italy, Easter was huge. I really remember the desserts—cannolis (on all the holidays), anisette cookies, Easter bread—shaped like a basket with eggs baked inside. My mom made breads in all different shapes. On Easter Sunday, we had to have new outfits; my mother would always stress over our outfits."

# The Easter Season: A Time of Religion and Renewal

As we know, Easter is the celebration of Jesus' death and resurrection. The Easter season commences with Ash Wednesday, which begins the season of Lent. During the forty days of Lent, there are several important days: Ash Wednesday, Palm Sunday, Holy Thursday, Good Friday, and Holy Saturday—all of which are religiously observed. Some Italian-Americans celebrate the beginning of Lent on Shrove Tuesday, the day before Ash Wednesday (which in Venice concludes Carnival), with Mardi Gras parties and huge feasts. Following is a brief description of the holy days of Easter.

## Ash Wednesday

On Ash Wednesday, priests use penitential ashes to make a sign of the cross on people's foreheads. Traditionally, the ashes come from burning the palm fronds from the previous year's Palm Sunday celebration. Catholics are advised not to eat meat on this day, which begins the season of Lent. On Ash Wednesday, Christians begin a period of sober reflection, self-examination, and spiritual redirection.

## Palm Sunday

Palm Sunday celebrates Jesus' journey into Jerusalem the week before his crucifixion. On this day Jesus rode a donkey and people greeted him by spreading palm branches on the road before him. Palm leaves are blessed and given out at mass on Palm Sunday, which also marks the beginning of Holy Week, the week preceding Easter.

## Holy Thursday

Holy Thursday was a traditional Jewish Passover feast. For Christians, it commemorates the Last Supper, which Jesus had with his disciples on the night before his crucifixion. During this feast, He left them with this message: Love each other.

## Good Friday

Good Friday is spent in spiritual meditation and penitence as Catholics remember Jesus' crucifixion. On this day, we somberly reflect on Jesus Christ's suffering and dying for our sins and therefore freeing us from damnation.

## Easter Sunday

Easter Sunday is the highlight of the season, on which Christians rejoice in Jesus' resurrection from the dead.

# Easter in Italy

In Italy, Easter (called *Pasqua*) presents many celebrations and festivals that vary from region to region and city to city. However, no matter where you go, you will find a huge Easter meal. While the contents of the Easter meal vary from region to region, some staples are eggs and dishes made with eggs, breads, and lamb—often a whole baby lamb roasted on an open fire. All of these carry symbolism in the Easter tradition.

In addition to observing the various religious days of the season by attending mass and praying, Italians spend Easter much as we do in the United States. They celebrate with family and friends, eat large meals with symbolic foods, and give gifts to loved ones.

Until recently, bunnies and many of the other icons Americans have come to associate with Easter have been hard to find in Italy. However, festive eggs have always had their place. In fact, throughout the country, beautiful chocolate eggs of varying sizes (from less than an ounce to nearly twenty pounds) are given to children and adults alike. And what makes them very special is that they (all but for the tiniest ones) have surprise gifts inside. These chocolate Easter eggs, called *uova di Pasqua*, are brightly wrapped hollow chocolate. The city of Perugia is renowned for its chocolate, and at Easter it offers a wide assortment of the chocolate eggs (and chickens).

In the 1400s, Italians started dying Easter eggs by staining them with flowers, herbs, and vegetables of different colors. For example, to color an egg purple, they would use violets; to turn it a golden hue, they used onions.

Other treats include an endless assortment of sweets—cookies, pastries, cakes, and *tortas*. Children enjoy a rich bread shaped like a crown and stuffed with colored Easter egg candies. Around the streets, the Easter season is noticeably in bloom, as shops display the fantastic treats and are decorated with colorful ribbons, bows, and spring flowers.

Holy Week is a somber time in Italy. Processions and Passion plays take place, portraying Jesus' death and resurrection. On the evening of Holy Thursday, people attend a special mass at which Christ's crucifixion is remembered. On Good Friday, in some towns people wearing hoods carry statues of the Passion of Christ around town in what is called "the Procession of the Mysteries." During this procession, the events of Christ's death are portrayed in great detail.

Easter Sunday is a very festive occasion, featuring special masses and elaborate feasts. On this day, Italians celebrate Jesus Christ's eternal life and the last of the three most important days in the Catholic year. Fabulous scents fill the streets as families prepare their delicious Easter dinners. One of the many special dishes of the day is *pizza ricresciuta* (or *rustica*), which is a pie filled with eggs, meats, and cheeses of all kinds. (In Rome, it is customary to have a priest bless the Easter meal before eating.)

Many families utilize the palms they received the previous Sunday (Palm Sunday) by dipping them into holy water and blessing everyone at the table. They also use the palms to create decorative items such as crosses.

In some places, a festival called "Scoppio del Carro" ("Explosion of the Cart") takes place. This event, dating back to the Crusades, features the explosion of a cart full of fireworks as large crowds gather to watch. In Florence, the "Scoppio del Carro" features an ornately decorated two-story cart pulled by white oxen and decorated with garland. The oxen pull the cart to a church in the town square, where they are cut loose and the fireworks are ignited. The tradition symbolizes the productivity of the harvest for the year to come. If the explosion is successful and powerful, it is seen as a good omen for the city, meaning that a productive harvest will follow. Then a parade (with decorations and costumes) takes place.

## Easter Monday

In Italy, the day after Easter, Easter Monday, or Pasquetta (meaning "Little Easter") is also a holiday, and it features even more feasting. People often celebrate this day, sometimes called Monday of Angels, with picnics, which often include roasted artichokes and other fresh vegetables, frittatas, salads, antipasto, meats (such as lamb, pork, and beef), bread, and wine.

## Carnival and Shrove Tuesday

Prior to the Easter season, Italians celebrate Carnival, a highly festive period that is well-known in Venice. Carnival concludes on Shrove Tuesday, the day before Ash Wednesday.

During Carnival, there are parades, wild displays of color and art, masquerades with elaborate masks and costumes, street performances, and intense celebration—eating, drinking, dancing, and rejoicing through the streets. Many sweets, such as the popular *sfrappole*, are eaten during this time.

Also sometimes referred to as Fat Tuesday, Shrove Tuesday is the last feast of the winter prior to the Lenten fast—the last opportunity to eat meat and dairy products. Traditionally, believers confessed their sins before the fast. Then they consumed the last of luxuries such as dairy foods and meat.

Originally, it was believed that if people confessed their sins on Shrove Tuesday, they would be absolved of them. In many Roman Catholic countries, Shrove Tuesday is the culminating day of Carnival, a word based on the Latin words *carne* ("meat") and *vale* ("farewell").

## The Italian-American Easter Menu

Traditional Italian Easter foods can be found in many varieties. Some carry over from different regions in Italy, and some are flavored with life in America and preference of individual cooks over the years. Many of the traditional dishes are prepared with eggs. Also common are dishes featuring lamb, goat and pig, sweets made with ricotta, and all sorts of bread, especially the overwhelmingly popular Easter bread with an egg or several eggs baked into it.

A traditional Easter breakfast might include a vegetable or ham-and-cheese frittata; or an omelet made with asparagus or broccoli, Italian sausage, mozzarella, ricotta, scamorza cheese, basil, parsley; hard-boiled eggs; bread, and sweets.

The afternoon meal (or dinner) usually features appetizers such as prosciutto and melon; antipasto bowls and platters featuring olives, artichoke hearts, peppers, salami, prosciutto, pimientos, and cheeses; or *antipasti misti* (Italian cold cuts, pickled vegetables, and pickled fish).

Italian Easter vegetable dishes include artichokes made different ways, such as fried (*carciofi fritti*), stuffed (*carciofi alla Romana*), and baked or sautéed with small potatoes (*carciofi e patate soffritti*); roasted peppers; *fagiolini al pomodora* (green bean casserole); sliced tomatoes topped with fresh parsley and garlic; and *finnobio*, stuffed zucchini flowers. There is also a wide range of salads, including *puntarelle* (a chicory salad with garlic dressing).

Italian Easter dinners often start with a soup, such as *brodetto Pasquale* (a broth-based soup made thick with eggs) or *minestra di Pasqua* (Easter soup), or a clear broth served with fried croutons (sometimes called *pancotta*).

Among the meats are lamb (*abbacchio*) in many forms: whole baby lamb, lamb shank, leg, or chops. It is prepared in many ways—over an open fire, roasted, fried, stewed, or cooked in fricassee sauce. Another popular meat is baby goat (*capretto*)—roasted with onions, potatoes, and seasonings; stewed; or cooked whole over an open-air spit. Dishes that feature goat include *capretto brodettato* (kid in a lemon sauce); cooked with artichoke (*carciofi*); *capretto al forno* (roasted); and *capretto caio e uova* (kid stewed with cheese, peas, and eggs). Other meats include ham, pork roast, turkey, and roast beef.

Pies and *tortas* made with meats and cheese are often featured at Italian-American Easter meals (either as the main course or on the side). Often called *pizza rustica*, prosciutto pie, and various *tortas*, these dishes are important symbols of Easter. They are often made with a thick crust and count sausage, ham, salami, prosciutto, and eggs among their ingredients. Different names and ingredient combinations vary according to different regional origins and families. For example, *a torta pasqualina* (from Liguria) is made with eggs, spinach, and ricotta; a dish from Calabria features ham, sausage, hard-boiled eggs, ricotta, and mozzarella; and one from Sicily includes macaroni, eggs, pork, and cheese.

Breads are a very important part of the Easter feast and are often presented very artistically. Feast breads, called *pani festivi*, include Easter egg bread (or Italian Easter Bread), a rich egg bread into which whole raw eggs are inserted into the braided dough, and the sweet Colomba Pasquale (one of the most popular breads from either Milan or Pavia), in which the dough is arranged in two pieces to look like a dove, and is then covered with crystalized sugar and whole unpeeled almonds.

Other Italian breads eaten at Easter include a bread from Marche called *crescia delle Marche*; an Easter cheese bread from Umbria called *crescia al formaggio*, which is made with a rich, briochelike dough and baked in a flowerpot; a sweet eggy bread from Rome called *pizza civita vecchia*, which contains ricotta, port or rum, and aniseed, and is slanted on the top; and the rich *gubana*, with nuts, dried fruit, spices, and liqueurs.

Easter sweets, called *dolci*, are abundant and include *pastiera di Pasqua* (Easter tart), lemon biscotti knots, Easter cake, ricotta cheesecake, ricotta pie, *cassata*, wheat pies (*La Pastiera a Napoletana*), panettone, Perugina chocolate, pies and *tortas* of many types, including *Pasqua torta* (sweetened ricotta pie flavored with lemon rind and cinnamon), as well as heaping trays of fruit (grapes, oranges, tangerines, pears, and figs). Sweets are served with coffee, espresso, and liqueurs.

## Symbolism

Easter carries with it various symbols, some of which are universal and others of which are specific to different cultures. Italians recognize many of these symbols, which are prominent in Easter celebrations. One of the foremost staples in an Italian Easter celebration is bread, which represents "the staff of life."

Eggs are commonly featured in Italian Easter feasts—eaten by themselves and used in many recipes—and contain a lot of symbolism. Eggs represent life, fertility, birth, beginnings, rebirth, spring, the beginning of a new year or season, and abundant life. Religiously, eggs symbolize Jesus' resurrection. It is said that it used to be forbidden to eat eggs during Lent and therefore they became a popular Easter food. Long ago, it was common for Christians to paint them and give them away as Easter gifts.

The lamb is another popular Easter symbol and is often used to represent Christ. An ancient belief was that the devil could turn himself into every other animal except a lamb (because of its religious affiliation). So, to see a lamb at Easter was considered good luck.

Other common Easter symbols include the pig, which represents good luck and prosperity (for example, piggy banks). Rabbits and hares are associated with fertility and throughout Europe symbolized abundant new life. The cross is the official symbol of Christianity and religious faith, and is a reminder that Jesus died by way of crucifixion. The Easter lily is a symbol of the new life of Jesus and His resurrection. It is commonly used in art, especially in stained-glass windows, as a reminder that all the events of Jesus' life point to his death and resurrection.

## Easter Activities

Easter presents the opportunity to engage in several fun activities. In my house we were never too old to color Easter eggs. Children and adults would sit together on evenings with dozens of cooled hard boiled eggs and coffee mugs filled with dyes. We also had clear wax with which to write names on eggs before dunking, and cardboard paper doll–type egg dressings. When we were finished we would scatter colored eggs around the house—adding them to bowls and decorations.

As a child, I also enjoyed making Easter baskets out of different materials, especially those green plastic strawberry baskets. Having our picture taken with the Easter bunny was another fun event.

# Decor

Easter decor is synonymous with springtime—greenery, flowers, pastel and bright colors, eggs, bunnies, baby animals, and cute things. Also used in Easter decor are stained glass, shiny foil materials, arches, crosses, and religious symbols.

My mom had several Easter decorations, although not nearly as many as for Christmas. I mostly remember the dining room table on Easter Sunday. It was set with a light green satin damask tablecloth and napkins, fine china (plates with a lace pattern around the edge and a pink rose in the center), and pale pink crystal wineglasses. The centerpiece was either an Easter tree—with white painted branches sprouting out several twigs covered with tiny plastic pastel eggs and silk flowers, and a bird in a nest—or a large ceramic rabbit sitting in the middle of the table on a nest of green Easter grass with colored Easter eggs scattered through it. There would also be an Easter basket holding the bread or rolls, pale pink satin ribbon tied around the crystal candleholders and the chandelier, and sometimes colored Easter eggs with each person's name painted on them as place settings. My mom also had various Easter serving dishes, such as a deviled egg plate with two little pig salt and pepper shakers in the middle.

# Incorporating Italian Easter Touches

Perugina chocolate Easter eggs with a surprise inside can be purchased at Italian delicatessens and bakeries. You can also order them from Italian Options, www.italianoptions.com. They carry "Large Chicken Eggs" (sugar-coated chocolate shells containing a surprise), sugar-coated chocolate mini eggs, and a variety of sugared almonds, chocolate dragées, and sugar balls. Kinder Eggs, www.kindermagicusa.com, features foil-wrapped chocolate eggs with little toys inside, including airplanes with rotating propellers and wheels, cars and trucks that roll, and animals with moving legs and heads.

To add more Italian touches to children's (and even adults') Easter baskets, consider vintage Italian toys (check eBay and various Internet sites as well as antiques and import stores). You can find toys from the 1920s through 1950s, including race cars, trucks, trains, fire brigades and gear, sleighs, electric trams and rail cars, ships, sailboats, eggcups, animals, carts, abacuses, blocks, games, puppets, wooden dolls, a variety of Pinocchios, hoops, tops, and rocking horses.

You can order Italian silver baby toys (car, airplane, motorcycle, and boat) from Favor Online, http://favoronline.safeshopper.com.

## Ideas for Easter Decorating

When decorating your home at Easter, and when setting an Easter table, you can use any of the beautiful flowers of spring, along with accents of ivy, palm fronds, ferns, and herbs as accents. Consider potted azaleas (in pink, red, and white), and arrangements using daisies, hydrangeas, peonies, tulips, garden roses, and orchids. Place a single white flower at each dinner guest's place setting. Place dainty flowers in antique eggcups (in silver, brass, or ceramic). Use Easter lilies in abundance for an Italian touch as well as for their beauty.

## Easter Recipes

### Frances Kaufmann's Easter Pie
#### (Pizza Rustica)

Crust *(makes 2 crusts; for 2 pies, makes 2 batches)*

2 cups all-purpose flour
1 teaspoon salt
4 egg yolks, from large eggs

1 pound butter, refrigerated and cut
    into 6 equal pats
⅓ cup ice water

## Filling *(makes enough for 2 pies)*

2 cups ricotta cheese
4 eggs, slightly beaten
1 pound cooked ham, diced into
   1-inch cubes
1 pound sausage, removed from
   casing and sautéed

5 hard-boiled eggs, sliced
2 tablespoons grated Romano
   cheese
1 cup fresh parsley, snipped
Salt and pepper to taste

In the bowl of a food processor, using the steel blade, spread flour and salt. Add 2 egg yolks. Scatter butter over flour. Process, turning machine on and off rapidly about five times until mixture is the size of peas. With machine running, add enough ice water through feed tube to have dough come together. Remove dough with floured hands. Shape into a ball. Wrap tightly in plastic wrap and chill in refrigerator for at least half an hour.

Preheat oven to 375 degrees. Gently mix filling ingredients together. Put aside. Roll out 2 crusts from each ball of dough. Place bottom crusts into 9-inch glass pie plates. Divide filling evenly into pie crusts. Moisten edge of bottom crusts with water. Cover with top crusts. Flute edges. Cut vent holes into top crust. Bake 35 to 40 minutes. Place on wire racks to cool. Beat 2 egg yolks. Brush top crusts with egg yolks. Cool completely. Lightly cover top with waxed paper. Store in refrigerator for up to a week.

# Mom's Bacon-and-Egg Pie

½ pound shortcrust pastry
½ pound bacon
3 eggs

5 ounces milk
Salt and pepper

Line a pie dish with pastry. Bake according to package directions (or at 400 degrees for 10 minutes or until lightly browned). Chop bacon and fry until brown. Arrange the fried bacon in the bottom of the pastry case. Beat the eggs and mix with milk and seasoning. Pour over the bacon. Cook at 350 degrees for 45 minutes, until risen and brown.

# Mediterranean Frittata

2 cups frozen Tuscan-style vegetables (broccoli, red peppers,
  mushrooms, onions)
1 cup onions, chopped
6 eggs

½ cup Parmesan cheese
1 teaspoon basil
1 teaspoon parsley
Salt and pepper to taste
2 tablespoons butter

Preheat oven to 350 degrees. Steam vegetables until tender, drain, and set aside. Sautée onion until tender. Beat eggs and add vegetables, sautéed onion, Parmesan, basil, parsley, salt, and pepper, and mix well. Heat butter in skillet and add egg mixture. Cook about 10 minutes over low to medium heat until mostly firm (except for the very top). Place the skillet in the oven and bake about 5 to 10 minutes, until top is set. Cut into wedges. (To make a Florentine frittata, substitute frozen vegetable mixture with 2 cups frozen chopped spinach, thawed, drained, and squeezed dry. You can also add ½ cup sliced red bell peppers and about half a cup of mozzarella, Swiss, or feta cheese. For another twist, use about 5 or 6 asparagus spears, halved crosswise, Parmesan cheese, 4 pieces of crumbled bacon, 1 cup white cheese of choice, and a dash of nutmeg.)

# Deviled Eggs

12 hard-boiled eggs, cooled
5 tablespoons mayonnaise
1 to 2 tablespoons Dijon mustard
½ cup onions, chopped

1 tablespoon parsley
1 teaspoon cayenne pepper
½ teaspoon salt
Paprika to garnish

Cut eggs in half lengthwise, remove yolks, and place yolks in large mixing bowl. Put egg whites on a platter and set aside. Mash the yolks with a fork, and mix with mayonnaise, mustard, onions, parsley, cayenne pepper, and salt. Spoon the mixture onto the egg white halves. Sprinkle paprika on top; chill. (For a more Italian-inspired twist, replace half of the mayonnaise with an equal amount of olive oil, and mix into egg mixture minced garlic, minced anchovies, basil, Parmesan cheese, chopped pepperoni, salami, or chopped black olives. Garnish with anchovy or sardine fillets, capers, Parmesan cheese, fresh basil leaves, olives, chopped artichoke hearts, peppers, or thinly sliced tomatoes.)

# Claro's Roasted Spring Lamb
# With Kalamata Olives

10 pounds fresh spring lamb, cut in
    roasting-size pieces
4 sprigs fresh oregano, stems removed
1 tablespoon fresh thyme, minced
¼ cup extra virgin olive oil

Salt and pepper to taste
8 cloves garlic
1 fresh onion, cut into quarters
2 cups dry white wine
1 cup kalamata olives, pitted

Preheat oven to 400 degrees. Season lamb with spices and olive oil. Toss to coat all pieces. Add garlic and onion to baking dish. Roast for about 20 minutes. Remove from oven, add wine, and toss to baste meat. Roast for about 20 more minutes. Remove and add olives and toss again. Continue roasting until meat is done, approximately 15 to 25 additional minutes, depending on size of lamb pieces.

# Claro's Baby Goat or Spring Lamb

12-to-15-pound baby goat or spring
    lamb
½ gallon white wine
1 cup lemon juice

½ cup chopped parsley
1 tablespoon rosemary, fresh or dry
Salt and pepper to taste
2 tablespoons garlic, finely chopped

Ask butcher to cut goat or lamb into serving pieces or quarters, as desired. Layer the pieces in a large roasting pan. To make the marinade, mix the wine, garlic lemon juice, parsley, and rosemary together and shake well. Pour this mixture over the meat and then lightly salt and pepper the meat. Leave it uncovered overnight in the refrigerator. The next day, cover the roasting pan with foil and bake in preheated 350-degree oven for 2 to 3 hours. Uncover and continue roasting for about 1 more hour, or until meat is done. To barbecue, cook slowly for about 2 hours, or until tender. Baste with extra marinade for a special old-fashioned treat!

# Sicilian Cassata

1 pound ricotta cheese
2 tablespoons heavy cream
2 tablespoons sugar

2 tablespoons orange liqueur
½ cup chopped walnuts, pistachios,
    or almonds

½ cup candied fruit, chopped
1 pound cake or sponge cake,
    cut into 4 horizontal pieces,
    for layering
½ cup semisweet chocolate, grated

Frosting, store-bought or home-
    made; or whipped cream or
    powdered sugar
Candied fruit, nuts, and chocolate,
    for topping

Mix cheese, cream, sugar, and liqueur. Fold in nuts, fruit, and chocolate. Layer cake with mixture and frost with chocolate frosting or whipped cream, or dust with powdered sugar. Top with candied fruit, nuts, and chocolate.

# Mini Calzones

2 tablespoons olive oil
2 cloves garlic, minced
1 whole medium white onion,
    chopped
½ cup (or 4 ounces) cream cheese
1 cup cottage cheese
¼ cup sour cream
1 package frozen chopped spinach
    (thawed, drained, and squeezed
    dry)
1½ cups shredded mozzarella
    cheese

1½ teaspoons garlic salt
1 teaspoon pepper
2 10-ounce cans of refrigerated
    pizza dough
Cooking spray
1 cup tomato sauce of choice
1 cup canned artichoke hearts,
    chopped
1 cup canned sliced mushrooms

Heat oil in skillet. Add garlic and onions and sauté until onions are softened (not browned). Remove from heat. In a large bowl, mix cream cheese, cottage cheese, and sour cream until smooth. Add spinach, 1 cup of mozzarella, garlic salt, and pepper, and mix well. Unroll pizza dough and spread out on flat surface. Split each dough into quarters (for a total of 8 smaller rectangles). Spray cookie sheets with cooking spray and place pieces of dough on sheets. On each piece of dough, spread a thin layer of tomato sauce on one half, then spinach and cheese mixture, followed by artichokes and mushroom slices. Sprinkle with mozzarella. Fold the other half over and pinch the ends closed (to seal edges). Bake according to directions on package, or until dough is lightly browned (about 15 minutes at 400 degrees).

# 13

# Italian Saints' Day Feasts and Other Feast Days

NUMEROUS SAINTS' FEAST DAYS are celebrated throughout the year in Italy, as well as by many Italian-Americans. Most people honor the patron saints of the regions from which they or their ancestors originated, or the saint for whom they were named. For example, people who descended from Bologna might pay tribute to St. Catherine on March 9 with a modest-to-elaborate celebration. A boy named Vincent (though his birthday might be in June) might receive gifts and a cake on September 27, the birthday of his namesake saint.

There are other saints whose feast days are popular celebrations for many, regardless of name or birthplace. For example, the feast day of St. John the Baptist is celebrated widely on June 24, with *nocino* (walnut liqueur), bruschetta, pasta, sausage, pork ribs, and snails. St. Anthony (of Padua) is honored on June 13 with songs written for him and with St. Anthony bread.

Saints' feast days can be acknowledged with a simple reflection or prayer, by attending mass, by placing flowers on or by a statue of the saint, by building an altar or shrine, or by setting out a statue or picture and maybe some candles. They can also be commemorated with an all-out feast featuring traditional foods, music, and revelry.

# Italians and the Saints

Patron saints are sometimes chosen as helpers or guardians over an aspect of life that is important to people, such as one's employment, health, interests, passion, marriage, emotional or spiritual state, or religious sacraments and institutions. For example, a person who loves or works with animals might have a special connection with St. Francis of Assisi, patron saint of animals.

Some patron saints are believed to be able to help people with certain illnesses or perils. St. Jude is the patron saint of desperate cases, and people often pray to him for help overcoming life-threatening diseases. St. Anthony, patron saint of lost items, is turned to for help in finding misplaced things.

With the majority of its population Roman Catholic, Italy celebrates the saints perhaps more than any other country. Even the smallest towns in Italy have patron saints, for whom celebrations, fairs, festivals, and pilgrimages are held each year. These events are very colorful, often featuring ornate decorations. Lights, candles, torches, and bonfires are lit. Fireworks are sometimes set off. Large feasts are prepared and shared with the entire community.

In the nineteenth century, Italian peasants threw huge feasts and parades in honor of their towns' patron saints to ensure that the saints would protect them from any disaster in the year to come. And although these people had few resources and lived modestly all year, they held back no expense during these elaborate celebrations.

The belief has been that saints have a direct line to God, so prayers and tributes to particular saints will be forwarded to God and therefore be heeded. It is believed that saints have powers of their own and can sway events, and that they are influential in helping prayers get answered.

Most cities honor their patron saints' days (*festa del patrono*) in the summer with celebrations that last for a couple of days or more, and usually feature processions (in which the saints' statues are carried through the streets) as well as fireworks, bonfires, confetti, traditional sweets, pageants, and festivals featuring booths with games and food.

# The Saints

Saints are martyrs who have been canonized by the Catholic Church, which determines that they have reached eternal glory. The Church decides that these people deserve public recognition for their role in interceding for us with the Lord, as well as for performing miracles. It is believed that prayers and offerings to the patron saint will persuade that saint to intervene with God to help people live life without harm.

# Major Saints' Days

Here is a brief overview of some of the popular saints that are celebrated. Of course, there are many more—one for almost any cause you can think of, as well as for every tiny town in Italy.

### St. John the Baptist (June 24)

The feast day of St. John the Baptist, also known as San Giovanni Battista, is celebrated by Italians everywhere, and especially in Rome, Turin, Florence, Genoa, Grello, and Spilamberto, as well as in the namesake town west of Naples.

St. John the Baptist is known for his courageousness, his direct teachings, and most of all, for baptizing Jesus Christ. He is associated with the sacrament of baptism—a very important rite of passage in the Catholic life—and therefore water.

John spoke out against cheating, adultery, greed, violence, and false accusations, and promoted charity, honesty, and justness.

The Society of St. John the Baptist organizes events in the saint's honor each year at Piazzale Michelangelo.

People make the walnut liqueur *nocino* in honor of St. John. In the region of Emilia-Romagna, on the evening of his feast day, several people venture into the woods to collect unripe walnuts with soft green shells in multiples of twenty-one, which represents three (for the Trinity) times seven (for the cardinal virtues). The nuts are crushed and alcohol is poured over them, followed by sugar and spices like cinnamon, cloves, and lemon rind. The concoction is left to sit for forty days, representing the number of days John the Baptist spent in the desert. Then it is sieved through cotton and drunk.

The feast often includes a snail feast called the *lumacata*—from a belief that eating snails protects against devils and witches—along with bread, such as saltless bread rolls called *panetti di San Giovanni* and bruschetta with garlic, olive oil, tomatoes, and mushrooms; pasta (including *ziti all San Giovanni*); pork; sausage; and white wine.

There are often barrels of water with yellow broom flowers, rose petals, and herbs floating in them. The following day, people wash their faces with the water to cleanse and purify the soul—thus keeping bad spirits away. This feast day ritual has been associated with the fermentation in wine. On the night of San Giovanni, people often say, *"La notte di San Giovanni entra il mosto nel chicco,"* which means "The must [grape juice] enters the grape seed." This saying is believed to begin the fermentation process.

Some Italian-Americans honor St. John the Baptist by sending each other roses, drinking *nocino*, and having a big feast with some of the traditional foods—pork, Italian sausage, ziti, and foccacia. Some ideas for honoring this feast day include floating rose and other flower petals in bowls of water and preparing a traditional feast with some of the foods mentioned above (including snails—*ala escargot*).

## San Gennaro (September 19)

San Gennaro is the patron saint of Naples. On his feast day, thousands of Neapolitans gather at the Treasure Chapel for a religious ceremony, Napoli Festival of San Gennaro, or La Festa di San Gennaro.

San Gennaro was Bishop of Benevento and was admired for being a protector and martyr. He was beheaded on September 19, A.D. 305. The legend is that after his death an old man found his body and head, gathered them, and wrapped them in a cloth. Then a woman collected his spilled blood and put it into two vials. Now two bottles filled with the saint's blood are kept at the Treasure Chapel, where on San Gennaro's feast day the blood transforms from the dry powdery substance to red "living" blood. This means that San Gennaro will continue for another year to protect Naples from natural disasters such as earthquakes, plagues, floods, and the eruption of Mount Vesuvius.

Since 1926, Italian-Americans in New York City's Little Italy have been honoring this saint with a huge eleven-day celebration on Mulberry Street. The street festival features music, dancing, games, and many street vendors selling all kinds of Italian foods—including sausage sandwiches and Italian pastries—as well as drinks and souvenirs.

## St. Francis of Assisi (October 4)

The feast day of St. Francis of Assisi is celebrated by many Italians, who remember him for his piety, sincerity, and the joy he brought to others.

St. Francis was the co-founder of the Franciscan order and the inventor of the Nativity scene. He is also known for his love, respect, oneness with nature, and ability to communicate with animals.

St. Francis was born in 1181, the son of a rich cloth merchant. He renounced his wealth and opted for a life of simplicity, poverty, and humility before God. He died on October 3, 1226, at the age of forty-four, half blind and extremely ill. He was canonized in 1228 by Pope Gregory IX.

It is said that St. Francis could talk to animals and that they listened to him. Stories about him include one in which he preached to hundreds of birds about thanking God "for their wonderful clothes, independence, and God's care." Another says he talked a wolf out of killing anyone ever again, and in fact the wolf became a pet and protector of the town.

St. Francis took care of the poor and lepers. He took the gospel of the Lord very literally and lived his life according to it. He had a stigmata (the markings of Jesus' wounds from the cross).

## St. Anthony of Padua (June 13)

St. Anthony of Padua's feast day is celebrated with feasts and ceremonies that include St. Anthony bread and singing a St. Anthony song.

St. Anthony was born into a wealthy family but renounced his wealth and became a Franciscan priest. He was a gifted speaker and a wonder worker, and was proclaimed a doctor of the Church.

St. Anthony is probably best known as the patron saint of lost items. The following prayer to him, if repeated enough, is said to help you find what you have lost: "Saint Anthony, St. Anthony, please come around, something is lost and can't be found. If you find it please bring it to me, and oh how happy I shall be."

## St. Lawrence (August 10)

St. Lawrence, or San Lorenzo, was a deacon, the patron saint of cooks, and was often portrayed with a grill. He was martyred by the Prefect of Rome in 258 C.E., tied to an iron grill and roasted alive while he prayed that the city of Rome would convert to Christianity. He is honored for giving to the poor.

## St. Catherine of Bologna (March 9)

St. Catherine of Bologna was born on September 8, 1413, the feast day of the Blessed Virgin Mary. St. Catherine was esteemed for her kindness, charity, and devotion to God.

At age eleven, she was appointed maid of honor to the Marquis of Ferrar's daughter, Princess Margarita, and received the same training and education. She studied fine arts and literature and later became a mystical writer. With God's inspiration, she wrote the book *The Seven Weapons Necessary for the Spiritual Combat.* She joined the Poor Clare convent, acting as the "doorkeeper."

St. Catherine was the first to recite the 1,000 Hail Marys on Christmas Eve (after Mary appeared to her and placed the Baby Jesus in her arms).

After her death, she was buried without a coffin or embalming. Because miracles kept occurring near her grave, her body was exhumed eighteen days after burial. Her body was incorrupt and smelled of sweet perfume. Her body remains incorrupt today in the Church of the Poor Clare convent in Bologna.

# List of Saints and Patronage

*San Antonio de Padua (St. Anthony)*—finding lost articles, for a good husband and for good fortune, of amputees, gravediggers, infertility, shipwrecks, starvation, sterility, faith in the blessed sacraments, animals, horses, harvests

*Santa Catalina de Bologna (St. Catherine of Bologna)*—artists and craftsmen, stenographers, secretaries, scribes, philosophers

*Santa Catalina de Siena (St. Catherine of Siena)*—nursing, health care, intelligent women, the tongue, fire, miscarriages, sexual temptation

*San Francisco de Asis (Francis of Assisi)*—the garden, small animals, human kindness, merchants, needleworkers, dying alone, fire, animal welfare societies, ecology, environmentalism, peace, zoos

*San Judas Tadeo (St. Jude)*—desperate cases and lost causes, desperation

*Santa Lucia (St. Lucy)*—optometrists, ophthalmologists, for good eyesight, blindness, peddlers, salesmen, writers

*San Lorenzo (St. Lawrence)*—restaurants, pasta, candy makers, dieters, lumbago (backache/back pain), cooks, fire, the poor, libraries

*San Nicholas*—Christmas, boys, bakers, brides, pawnbrokers, brewers, children

*St. Stephen (the first martyr)*—bricklayers, headaches, horses

*St. John the Baptist*—convulsions, epilepsy, hailstorms, spasms, baptism, monastic life

*St. Clare of Assisi*—eye disease, telegraphs, telephones, television

## St. Catherine of Siena (April 29)

Born in Siena on March 25, 1347, St. Catherine of Siena was called Patroness of Italy and a Doctor of the Church. She started seeing visions at a young age, and later underwent the mystic experience of "spiritual espousals."

St. Catherine tended to the poor and the sick, especially those with hideous diseases. She became a Dominican Tertiary at sixteen, and continued to have visions of Christ, Mary, and the saints. In 1375, she received stigmata, but the marks weren't visible until after she died in Rome on April 29, 1380, at the age of thirty-three. Her body was found incorrupt in 1430.

# Partial List of Saints' Feast Days (by Month)

## January
17—St. Anthony
20—St. Fabian and
    St. Sebastian
21—St. Agnes
22—St. Vincent
24—St. Frances de Sales
26—St. Timothy and
    St. Titus

## February
5—St. Agatha

## March
4—St. Casimir
7—St. Perpetua and
    St. Felicity
9—St. Frances of Rome
17—St. Patrick
19—St. Joseph
23—St. Turibius

## April
7—St. John Baptist
    de la Salle
11—St. Stanislaus
13—St. Martin I

## May
3—St. Philip and St. James
12—St. Nereus and
    St. Achilleus
20—St. Bernadine
    of Siena
25—St. Bede the Venerable, St. Gregory VII, and St. Mary Magdalene de' Pazzi
26—St. Phillip Neri
27—St. Augustine

## June
2—St. Marcellinus and
    St. Peter
13—St. Anthony of Padua
24—St. John the Baptist
29—St. Peter and St. Paul

## July
3—St. Thomas
11—St. Benedict
13—St. Henry
15—St. Bonaventure
22—St. Mary Magdalene
25—St. James
26—St. Joachim and
    St. Anne
29—St. Martha

## August
8—St. Dominic
10—St. Lawrence and St. Clare
24—St. Bartholomew

## September
16—St. Cornelius and
    St. Cyprian
19—St. Januarius
21—St. Matthew
26—St. Cosmas and
    St. Damian
27—St. Vincent de Paul

## October
4—St. Francis of Assisi
6—St. Bruno
9—St. Denis
18—St. Luke
29—St. Paul of the Cross
23—St. John of Capistrano
28—St. Simon and St. Jude

## November
3—St. Martin de Porres
10—St. Leo the Great
15—St. Albert the Great
16—St. Gertrude the Great
22—St. Cecilia
23—St. Clement I and
    St. Columban
30—St. Andrew

## December
6—St. Nicholas
7—St. Ambrose
13—St. Lucy
26—St. Stephen

## Events Honoring Patron Saints in Italy

January 17, Naples: Festa d'o'Cippo di Sant'Antonio. A procession for St. Anthony, protector of animals.

April 25, Venice: Festa di San Marco. Festival honoring Venice's patron saint (St. Mark), with gondola race across St. Mark's Basin.

May 6, Cocullo, Abruzzo: Festa di San Domenico Abate. Includes a procession with a statue of St. Dominic covered with live snakes.

Mid-June through mid-July, Turin, Piedmont: Festa di San Giovanni (the city's patron saint, John). A festival held since the fourteenth century.

June 27, Amalfi, Campania: Festa di Sant Andrea (St. Andrea). Features fireworks and processions.

July 16, Naples: Festa della Santa Maria del Carmine. Features a festival and illumination of the Campanile bell tower.

September 3, Viterbo, Lazio: Procession of the Macchina di Santa Rosa. Commemoration of the saint's body's being transported to the Church of Santa Rosa in the 1200s.

September 19, Naples: The Miracle of San Gennaro. Mass features the reenactment of the liquefaction of the saint's blood.

October 4, Assisi, Umbria: Festa di San Francesco. Feast in honor of St. Francis of Assisi.

November 21, Venice: Festa della Salute. Feast of thanks for the Virgin Mary's saving people from the plague in 1630.

## More Italian Holidays and Feasts

In addition to the many saints' feast day celebrations that take place throughout the year all over Italy, there are several more festivities commemorating important religious events and other events.

## The Feast of the Assumption of Mary

The Feast of Mary's Assumption into Heaven, also referred to as Ferragosto, is celebrated on August 15 all over Italy. This feast day honors the death, assumption, and coronation of the Blessed Virgin Mary. It is the biggest Italian holiday in the summer, and features a variety of fairs, festivals, religious services, and processions. In many small Italian towns, plays portraying the miracle also take place.

Ferragosto was introduced by Caesar Augustus as *Feriae Augusti*, meaning "the summer holiday of Augustus." It was later merged with religious celebrations and called the Feast of the Assumption. On this day, people commemorated the taking of the Virgin Mary's body into heaven. It is believed that Mary's body (not subject to decay) was taken into heaven to be reunited with her soul.

Beautiful paintings depicting this miraculous event can be seen in different Italian cities. Antonio da Correggio's fresco *Assumption of the Virgin* (1534) floats up the Romanesque *duomo* on Piazza Duomo in Parma, in the region of Emilia-Romagna. In the Santa Maria Gloriosa dei Frari, a huge Gothic church in Venice, Titian's magnificent *Assumption of the Virgin* backs the altar.

Assumption celebrations can also be found in towns around the United States. For example, each year in Cleveland's Little Italy, a neighborhood celebration lasting several days features all kinds of Italian food for sale at booths as well as entertainment, including musicians and bands playing Italian classics, Bingo, carnival games, and rides. On the day of the Assumption there is a mass, followed by a procession of the statue of the Virgin Mary through the streets. The day concludes with the firing of a cannon and fireworks.

## Other Festivals

*Sagre* are festivals or fairs (mostly taking place in the summer) in Italy that various cities and towns host in honor of a particular food. *Sagre* are held for spaghetti, wine, mushrooms, tomatoes, gelato (ice cream), and many types of fruit. During these celebrations hundreds, sometimes thou-

## Sagre Events in Italy

Mid-March, in Madonna di Campiglio, Trentino-Alto Adige: Mostra Vini Spumanti. A fair celebrating sparkling wine.

Late May, in Ora, Trentino-Alto Adige: Festa della Mela. "Festival of the Apple."

June 1, Borgo San Martino, Alessandria: Festa della Fragola. "Celebration of the Strawberry," with musical and folkloric performances.

Early September, in Rome: Sagra dell'Uva. A festival with grapes at harvest, with folk entertainment.

Second week of September, in Chianti, Tuscany: Rassegna del Chianti Classico. A celebration of local wines.

First Sunday of October, Alba, Piedmont: Fiera del Tartufo. Several events centered around locally grown white truffles.

First week of October, Castelli, Romani, Lazio. Wine festivals.

October (date varies), in Bolzano, Trentino-Alto Adige: Festa dell'Uva. Grape festival with lively music and processions.

sands, of people—townspeople and tourists—gather to feast on the food being honored, which is also often accompanied by pasta and other dishes, music, and dancing. Bonfires, fireworks, and elaborate pageants are also often featured.

In addition to *Sagre*, Italy is buzzing all year long with festivals devoted to the arts, sports, and other events. Some examples include Tuscany's most famous event, Corsa del Palio, held in Siena on July 2. This day features medieval flag waving and horse racing. Pisa's Luminaria, Festival of Lights, is held on June 16 and 17. Maggio Musicale is held in Florence from May to June, and Venice's Biennale, from June through September, is the world's biggest exhibition of contemporary art.

# 14

# Sunday Dinners and Other Special Occasions

GROWING UP IN AN ITALIAN-AMERICAN FAMILY, I learned that family was the most important thing in life and that any celebration was to be spent with them. All events—birthdays, anniversaries, Mother's Days, Father's Days, and even Sundays—were reasons to celebrate. Much like the holidays already discussed, these occasions also featured big meals with lots of courses.

For most traditional Italian-American families, the term "Sunday dinners" is very familiar. They recall, and often still participate in, big dinners on Sunday evenings with the whole family. Everyone is expected to be there. Whether the group consists of just the immediate family or includes extended family and sometimes close friends, it is highly unlikely for any of the usual group to miss it.

It's usually a casual affair when everyone can unwind and have a little fun and a great meal before the new week begins. For many families the meal is Italian, with some kind of pasta dish; rich sauce; meatballs, sausage, or sometimes meat like chicken, beef, or pork roast; vegetables; salad; bread; wine; dessert, and coffee.

At my parents' house, Sunday dinners started with wine and appetizers around the kitchen counter. The appetizers were simple, such as chips and dips or salsa, pretzels, nuts, and sometimes pizza or foccacia. Then dinner was held in the dining room or out on the patio and ranged from barbecue chicken or steak with Dad's famous home fries, rice or baked potatoes, steamed vegetables (broccoli and asparagus), salad and rolls, to spaghetti and Mom's wonderful meatballs or Crockpot chicken cacciatore, garlic bread, and salad. Wine was always on the table, and there was often at least one bottle of white and one red open at all times. After dinner, there was plenty of dessert—any kind of pie, Italian cookies and pastries on a platter, lemon cake, or ice cream.

As a child, these dinners didn't seem like a big deal. It was just the normal thing to do on Sunday evenings. But as I got older, I started to see how special they were and how fortunate I was to have a family who liked to get together so much. None of my non-Italian-American friends did this, at least not to this extent.

As an adult I came to look forward to these Sunday dinners at my parents' house. The routine was almost therapeutic. I could always count on the same people to be there, and things to go the same way: Mom and Dad cooking in the kitchen, everyone gathering at the counter, a big meal and a relaxed environment. My husband started looking forward to it as well. Although he too is Italian-American, his immediate family doesn't follow many of the traditions.


# Sunday Dinner Reflections

### Ernestine Levinson

"My father, who was born in Tuscany, was a hunter-gatherer, and a great cook. During summers, which my family spent on my uncle's upstate farm, he would hunt deer, rabbits, and small birds; catch frogs, gather snails, fish for trout, forage for mushrooms and wild dandelions, and farm fresh vegetables, such as corn, tomatoes, and eggplant. Much of this bounty would end up on both our summer and winter Sunday dinner tables. The tomatoes, which my father raised, would be dried, along with the mush-rooms, and then be added to the sauces for traditional Italian dishes.

"Since I was an only child and my father was more suited to being the parent of a son, he would take me with him to forage, hunt, and fish. He taught me how to use a rifle when I was ten, and also taught me to iden-tify edible mushrooms from poisonous ones at about the same time. I never thought to question my father's mushroom expertise. In retrospect, I assumed he knew what he was doing since all who ate his mushrooms had survived. However, I have never trusted my own knowledge and gave up mushroom hunting years ago much to my husband's relief. Actu-ally he still eyes with suspicion any mushrooms that I serve him.

"In our home, my mother, who was American-born but of Southern Italian background, would cook the weekday meals of mostly American food with a touch of Italian. But for Sunday dinner it was my father's chance to shine and show off his culinary talents. Homemade fettuccini, linguini, or spinach-and-cream-cheese-stuffed ravioli would be rolled out and made the night before and left overnight to dry. Then on Sunday morning my father would rise early and start the sauce (or "gravy" as we called it). Into it would go sausage, *braciole* (stuffed rolled beef), chicken legs, meatballs, and the aforementioned dried mushrooms and sun-dried tomatoes (now a pricey, trendy, food). The sauce would then simmer for about five or six hours.

"Our Sunday dinners were large affairs with many invited friends and relatives. First there would be an antipasto consisting of various salamis, provolone, fresh mozzarella cheese, olives, anchovies, celery, and roasted peppers served with crusty Italian bread. Then out would come the great pasta dish followed by the meats cooked in the sauce. Were we finished? No! Next we'd have a roast with potatoes, vegetables, and salad. Finally there was fresh fruit and demitasse coffee laced with anisette. Sweets (*dolci*) were reserved for holidays and special occasions.

"In my home there were often loud arguments over the merits of Southern Italian cooking versus Northern Italian cooking. I, of course, was the beneficiary of this rivalry, which resulted in cooking contests with one meal better than the last. Despite being plied with all this food, I managed to remain painfully thin. When a school nurse was sent to my home to see if I was being properly fed, she was ushered in by my mortified mother who showed her the array of food cooking on the stove and invited her to stay for dinner. The nurse never returned, accepting the explanation for my scrawniness as genetic.

"The obligatory Sunday dinners continued into my adulthood, marriage, and parenthood years. There were times when I felt stifled and trapped by family obligations. I yearned to spend my Sundays in athletic or cultural pursuits and I was often annoyed that I could not travel during holidays, but had to be home to celebrate with family.

"After my parents died, I slowly began to enjoy the freedom of my weekends and I started to experiment with the tastes of different and exotic cuisines, such as those of India, Mexico, and the various regions of China.

"With a husband who prefers playing the piano and tennis to cooking, and a busy volunteer, learning, and social schedule myself, we now eat lighter and healthier meals than my parents did. But I'm aware that people are now paying outrageous prices in restaurants to eat the pesto, polentas, and risottos that were my soul food when I was growing up.

"Although I am an above average cook, I lack the patience, inclination, and energy to duplicate those special Sunday feasts. More often than not we eat out now on Sundays and when my husband asks me where I want to eat, it isn't Chinese, Indian, or Mexican I yearn for anymore, but a good Italian meal. It's as if I'm on an endless search for the tastes of my childhood. They say you can't go home again, and I know that it's true, but how I wish I could go home again just one more time for one of Daddy's special Italian Sunday dinners."

## Dorothy Pantleo

"It's very important to me to hold on to these traditions. My husband and I and our kids enjoy it. My husband and I are of the same background, and it was important in his family too to keep up the traditions. That's what keeps it going. Now we have spaghetti and sauce every Sunday. It is our gathering time."

# Mother's Day and Father's Day Celebrations

For many Italian-Americans, Mother's and Father's Days are almost as big as Easter and Christmas (without the religious aspect). We would never dream of missing an opportunity to celebrate our parents, with a feast in their honor, followed by cake and special gifts.

Because these days always fall on Sundays, our family would get together for a slightly bigger feast than the typical Sunday dinner. The guests of honor would be all the mothers—my mom, aunt, and grand-mothers—or all the fathers. Each honored guest would receive gifts, and all the preparations, serving, and cleanup would be done by the non-mothers or non-fathers.

## Mother's Day

Mother's Day (*Festa della Mamma*) has been celebrated around the world for as long as anyone can remember. In prehistoric times, people hon-ored the "Great Mother," which represented fertility. Later, different coun-tries and cultures came up with their own ways to commemorate this day. The Romans honored the goddess Cybele with banquets for a week in May. The celebrations were named "Floralia" and were dedicated to flow-ers and springtime. Now in Italy, like in the United States, Mother's Day is celebrated on the second Sunday in May.

Family is the strongest Italian institution, and serves as a source of protection and support. The Italian mother is the center of the family, often holding families together. In many traditional Italian-American fami-lies, mothers do most of the cooking and housework. So on Mother's Day, it's important to make sure she doesn't have to do anything. One way to ensure this is to take her out to brunch or dinner. Or have her to your house, or bring a fully prepared meal to her. Just don't let her jump up and try to help. Perhaps you might prepare a favorite recipe of hers that she taught or passed down to you.

For Mother's Day gifts, flowers have always been a popular choice. However, I like to give Mom something more personal. For the past few years, it has become a tradition for me to go to a local spa and buy two gift certificates for European facials, and give one to my mom for Mother's Day. Then in the next few weeks, we choose a day to go have lunch and have facials together.

### Father's Day

For most Italians in Italy, Father's Day is celebrated on St. Joseph's Day. However, Italian-Americans celebrate it in June. Again a large feast is prepared in Dad's honor, followed by a special cake and gifts.

My dad didn't care too much about Father's Day, about being the guest of honor and receiving gifts. For him, it was enough just to have the family there for the usual Sunday dinner. For the last five years, he was the only guest of honor as the grandfathers had already passed away, and there were no other fathers there. He gratefully opened his gifts and accepted his moment in the spotlight.

## Adding Italian Touches to Other Holidays and Celebrations

You can add Italian touches to any holiday, special occasion, or party. The main way to do this is with the food served—either the entire menu or certain dishes. For example, for a birthday party, you might make (or buy) an Italian birthday cake, Sicilian *cassata*, or tiramisu. For a summertime barbecue you might grill Italian sausage and serve it with rolls and spaghetti.

You can also incorporate things like music, decorations, gifts, favors, or activities to give your celebration an Italian feel. For Valentine's Day, there is a CD called "Italian Love Songs," produced by EMI Music/ Special Markets, that features several Italian and Italian-American artists singing such titles as "That's Amore." The CD includes two disks filled with hits by Al Martino, Connie Francis, Dean Martin, Julius La Rosa, Luciano Pavarotti, and more.

For a birthday, play the Italian version of the song "Happy Birthday." Fun birthday parties can also be held at quaint little family-run Italian restaurants. Italian chain restaurants, especially Bucca di Beppo, also make for fun birthday spots.

Fun activities for certain events, such as picnics and barbecues, include playing boccie ball or soccer. Playing cards, doing traditional dances like the tarantella, or watching Italian movies are some other ideas.

For an Italian Valentine, put together a gift basket featuring such romantic items as Italian cookies, almond biscotti, Italian hard candies, Perugina chocolates, the "Italian Love Songs" CD, a romantic movie such as *Moonstruck, Roman Holiday,* or *Mickey Blue Eyes,* pistachios, almonds, roasted cashews, and packets of gourmet cappuccino.

Add Italian touches to St. Patrick's Day by serving green Italian foods, such as green linguine or tortellini stuffed with spinach with a spinach pesto sauce, green beans, peas, broccoli, asparagus, green peppers, or herbed foccacia (with basil and parsley). For fun, display a pot of gold chocolate coins, make shamrock-shaped sugar cookies, frosted with green frosting, or set out bowls of green Jordan almonds.

# Recipes

## Cheesy Bread Rounds

12 slices white or whole-wheat
   bread
1 cup cottage cheese

½ cup Parmesan cheese
6 slices peppered salami, chopped

Cut out a circle in the bread slices of desired size using the rim of a wine glass or cookie cutter (or cut into small squares, triangles, or other shapes). Lightly toast bread. Preheat oven to 350 degrees. Mix cottage cheese and parmesan cheese in a bowl. Spoon cheese mixture on bread pieces and sprinkle salami on top. Bake for about 15 minutes (until cheese melts and starts to bubble).

# Eggplant Garlic Bread Sandwiches

¼ cup butter, softened
¼ cup sour cream
2 cloves garlic, minced
6 French rolls
1 cup bread crumbs
½ cup Parmesan cheese
2 eggs, beaten

2 tablespoons olive oil
2 large (or 3 medium) eggplants, cut
  into half-inch slices
2 tomatoes, thinly sliced
2 onions, thinly sliced
1 cup spaghetti sauce
12 thin slices of mozzarella cheese

Mix softened butter, sour cream, and garlic. Cut rolls in half and spread with garlic mixture. Place in broiler about 5 to 7 minutes (until just golden brown). Remove and set aside. Preheat oven to 350 degrees. Mix bread crumbs and Parmesan cheese. Beat eggs in a separate bowl. Dip eggplant slices into eggs and then into bread crumbs, coating all over. Heat olive oil in skillet and cook eggplant until lightly browned. Place French roll halves on baking sheet and layer every other piece with two pieces eggplant, tomato, and onion and drizzle with sauce. Bake uncovered for about 20 minutes. (You may need to remove the garlic bread pieces without toppings.) Add mozzarella slices on top of sauce and bake an additional 5 minutes (or until cheese melts). Assemble sandwiches and serve.

# Mom's Stuffed Shells

## Sauce

1½ cups onion, finely chopped
3 cloves garlic, crushed
⅓ cup olive oil
2 29-ounce cans of Italian tomatoes
1 6-ounce can tomato paste
3 tablespoons fresh parsley,
  chopped

1 tablespoon salt
1 tablespoon sugar
1 teaspoon dried oregano leaves
1 teaspoon dried basil leaves
¼ teaspoon pepper
1½ cups water

Saute onion and garlic in hot oil for 5 minutes. Mix in rest of the ingredients. Bring to a boil and reduce heat. Cover and simmer 1 hour, stirring occasionally.

## Filling

1 package large pasta shells
2 pounds ricotta cheese
1 8-ounce package mozzarella
    cheese, diced or shredded
1½ cups Parmesan or Romano
    grated cheese

2 eggs
1 teaspoon salt
¼ teaspoon pepper
1 tablespoon chopped parsley

Boil large pasta shells until just tender. Drain and rinse carefully (trying not to break).

Preheat oven to 350 degrees. In large bowl, combine ricotta, mozzarella, ⅓ cup parmesan or romano, eggs, salt, pepper, and parsley. Beat with wooden spoon to blend well. Spoon about ¼ cup of filling into each shell. Spoon 1 ½ cups sauce onto the bottom of two large baking dishes. Place shells topside up in a single layer on pans. Top with more sauce and sprinkle with remaining Parmesan or Romano cheese. Bake uncovered ½ hour or until bubbly.

## Mom's Braciola

1½ pounds round steak, cut about a
    half inch thick
2 cloves garlic, sliced
2 teaspoons Parmesan cheese
1 teaspoon parsley
2 slices bacon, cut into small pieces
¼ cup raisins
¼ cup pine nuts

1 teaspoon salt
½ pepper
¼ cup olive oil
1 small onion, sliced
2½ cups chopped tomatoes
½ cup red wine
1 teaspoon brown sugar
1 bay leaf

Lay out steak pieces and top with garlic, Parmesan cheese, parsley, bacon, raisins, pine nuts, ½ teaspoon salt, and ¼ teaspoon pepper. Roll and tie shut. Heat olive oil in skillet. Add onions and cook until softened. Add steak rolls and brown all over. Mix together tomatoes, wine, brown sugar, ½ teaspoon salt, ¼ teaspoon pepper, and bay leaf. Add sauce to skillet. Cover and simmer about an hour (until steak is tender). Remove string and bay leaf. Slice and serve.

# Italian Chicken Strips

4 large skinless, boneless chicken
    breasts, cut into strips
2 to 4 cups white wine
2 to 3 cloves garlic, sliced
1 cup flour

1 teaspoon salt
½ teaspoon pepper
1 teaspoon basil
1 tablespoon Parmesan cheese
2 tablespoons (or more) olive oil

Marinate chicken strips in wine and garlic slices at least one hour (preferably overnight). Mix flour, salt, pepper, basil, and Parmesan cheese in bowl. Dip chicken strips in this mixture and coat. Heat oil in skillet. Add chicken strips and cook to golden brown, turning often (about 10 minutes) until cooked through. Serve alone or with pasta.

# Acknowledgments

I WOULD LIKE TO THANK the many people who contributed to this book, via content, professional services, and support.

Thank you to all the Italian-Americans who shared your stories and contributed your recipes: Josie Vinci, Dorothy Pantleo, Professor Philip Di Novo, Diane Reid, Tery Spataro, Joyce Spataro, David Manzari, Sederina (Rina) Mele and the Bella Italia family, Sandi Bastianelli, Grace Bastianelli, Judge Alfred J. DiBona, Jean A. DiBona, Mary Fanara, Mary Linda Daddona, Rosemarie Lippman and the entire Claro's staff (specifically Angela Cafaro, Lucia, and Rosalia), Michael Granieri, Regina Buzzello, Frances Gendimenico Kaufmann, Ernestine Levinson, Gina (Corigliano) Schaffer, Ginny (Granieri) Craven, Barbara Lando Stead, Michelle and Aimee Stead, and my many Italian ancestors.

For your professional services, I thank Jonathan Michaels, Richard Williams, LaVonne (Mimi) Marino, Bruce Bender, Margaret Wolf, Francine Hornberger, and the staff at Kensington Books and Citadel Press.

For your continued love and support, I am forever thankful to my mom, Toni (Marino) Mutz, my husband, Bobby Granieri, and all my family and friends (and Kensi, too).

# Index

Uncle Vic's Gnocchi, 160
*Uova di Pasqua*, 184, 190
Urn of Fate, 71, 110–11

Valentine's Day, 212, 213
Veal Cutlets
    in Lemon Sauce, Claro's,
        161
    with Mushrooms and Marsala
        Wine, Claro's, 160–61
Vegetable(s), 128–29. *See also*
        Eggplant; Stuffed Peppers
    Fried Cardune, Claro's, 138
    Garlic Mashed Potatoes, 39
    Pasta with Roasted, 22
    Pepper-Stuffed Tomatoes, 36
    served at Christmas, 118
    served at Easter, 187
    served St. Joseph's Day, 167,
        168
    Stuffed Artichokes, LaVonne
        Marino's, 35
    Stuffed Mushrooms, 32

Stuffed Onions, 35
    Zucchini Fans, Claro's, 38
Venice, saints' feast days in, 204
Venetian Gondola Christmas
        Decoration (craft project),
        88
Villages, miniature. *See* Little
        villages
Vinci, Josie
    on Christmas, 63–64
    on New Year's Eve, 147
    on St. Joseph's Day, 169
Vineyard Tabletop Christmas
        Tree (craft project), 86
Virgin Mary, festivals honoring,
        6, 42, 49–50, 205

Walnuts, St. John and, 198–99
When the Clock Strikes 12 New
        Year's Eve party theme, 152
Wine
    Claro's Sausage with Peppers,
        Onions, and, 162

Cream Sauce, Pasta with,
        Gina Schaffer's, 137
    *sagre* and, 2066
    serving at Christmas, 122–25
    serving at Thanksgiving, 31
    serving New Year's Eve, 156
Wine parties, for Christmas, 98
Winter solstice. *See* Saturnalia
Winter Wonderland Christmas
        party theme, 100
Wrapping Christmas gifts,
        108–9
Wreaths
    Advent, 47–48, 85
    Christmas, 84

Yule. *See* Saturnalia
Yule logs, 57

*Zampone*, 155
Zeppole, 168, 170, 171
    St. Joseph's Day (recipe), 174
Zucchini Fans, Claro's, 38